*American Diplomacy
during the Second World War,
1941-1945*

American Diplomacy during the Second World War, 1941-1945

GADDIS SMITH
Yale University

John Wiley and Sons, Inc., New York · London · Sydney

2108

Foreword

"THE UNITED STATES always wins the war and loses the peace," runs a persistent popular complaint. Neither part of the statement is accurate. The United States barely escaped the War of 1812 with its territory intact, and in Korea in the 1950's the nation was forced to settle for a stalemate on the battlefield. At Paris in 1782, and again in 1898, American negotiators drove hard bargains to win notable diplomatic victories. Yet the myth persists, along with the equally erroneous American belief that we are a peaceful people. Our history is studded with conflict and violence. From the Revolution to the Cold War, Americans have been willing to fight for their interests, their beliefs, and their ambitions. The United States has gone to war for many objectives — for independence in 1775, for honor and trade in 1812, for territory in 1846, for humanity and empire in 1898, for neutral rights in 1917, and for national security in 1941. Since 1945 the nation has been engaged in a deadly struggle to contain communism and defend the democratic way of life.

The purpose of this series is to examine in detail eight critical periods relating to American involvement in foreign war from the Revolution through the Cold War. Each author has set out to recount anew the breakdown of diplomacy that led to war and the subsequent quest for peace. The emphasis is on foreign policy, and no effort is made to chronicle the military participation of the United States in these wars. Instead the authors focus on the day-by-day conduct of diplomacy to explain why the nation went to war and to show how peace was restored. Each volume is a synthesis combining the research of other historians with new insights to provide a fresh interpretation of a critical period in

American diplomatic history. It is hoped that this series will help dispel the illusion of national innocence and give Americans a better appreciation of their country's role in war and peace.

ROBERT A. DIVINE

Preface

U NLIKE SO MUCH of the writing on the diplomacy of the Second World War, this book is not a study of the origins of Soviet-American antagonism. It is an attempt to treat of the diplomatic events of 1941–1945 in terms of the themes which American leaders at the time considered significant. I have sought to remove myself as far as possible from a present overpowering awareness of the Cold War in order to approach the past from the point of view of the men who participated in the events about which I write.

I have many people to thank for helping make this book possible: Robert A. Divine for his invitation to write this book and for his expert criticism; William Gum of John Wiley and Sons for his genial encouragement; Nancy Unger and Judith Starnes of John Wiley and Sons for their editorial talents; Miriam Swanson for her competence at the typewriter; my wife for her cheerful acceptance of the chaos which writing a book brings to a household and for her invaluable day-by-day critical comments; my students, in particular Carter Findley and Wilton B. Fowler, for listening patiently and critically; my colleagues in teaching diplomatic history for their provocative conversation, Claude E. Barfield, Jr., George Langdon, Nicholas X. Rizopoulos, Robert E. Wall, and Harold B. Whiteman, Jr.; colleagues in other fields for sharing their special knowledge, William Roger Louis and Warren M. Tsuneishi; my brother, Samuel Wood Smith, in Calcutta for criticizing Chapter 5; and Samuel Flagg Bemis, Sterling Professor Emeritus of Diplomatic History, for continuing to be my teacher. Finally, I acknowledge my debt to the dozens of scholars whose books introduced and guided me through the complex events of 1941–1945. My footnotes and bibliography give their names, but fail to express the measure of my admiration and appreciation for their labors.

GADDIS SMITH

New Haven, Connecticut
October 1964

Contents

MAPS

(All maps by Theodore R. Miller)

American Diplomacy
during the Second World War,
1941–1945

PRINCIPAL WARTIME CONFERENCES, 1941–1945

December 24, 1941–January 12, 1942 Washington, D. C. (ARCADIA): Churchill, Roosevelt, and staffs for strategic planning.

January 14–23, 1943 Casablanca, Morocco: Churchill, Roosevelt, and military advisers. "Unconditional surrender" announced.

May 12–23, 1943 Washington, D. C. (TRIDENT): Churchill, Roosevelt, and staffs for strategic planning.

August 14–24, 1943 Quebec, Canada (QUADRANT): Churchill, Roosevelt, and military advisers. Cross-Channel invasion plans made firm.

October 19–30, 1943 Moscow, U.S.S.R.: American, British, and Soviet foreign ministers. Russia agrees in principle to a postwar world security organization.

November 22–December 7, 1943 Cairo, Egypt (SEXTANT) and Teheran, Iran: Roosevelt, Churchill, and Chiang Kai-shek at Cairo; Roosevelt, Churchill, and Stalin at Teheran. First Big Three meeting.

September 12–16, 1944 Quebec, Canada: Roosevelt, Churchill, and advisers. Morgenthau plan for Germany discussed.

February 4–9, 1945 Yalta, U.S.S.R.: Roosevelt, Churchill, and Stalin with staffs. Extensive planning for postwar Europe and Asia.

July 16–26, 1945 Potsdam, Germany: Truman, Churchill and Atlee, and Stalin with staffs. Inconclusive discussions. Japan warned to surrender. First atomic bomb tested just before conference convenes.

CHAPTER I

The Nature of Wartime Diplomacy

IN THE FIRST HALF of the twentieth century man approximately doubled his population, quadrupled his industrial production, and radically altered the form of government over most of the earth. He also increased a thousandfold his power to kill. Chronic, dangerous instability was the result. World security depended as never before on international cooperation, but suspicion and hostility were the rule between states. Some nations longed for peace but prepared fearfully for war. Other nations gloried in the use of force because amoral leaders preferred to steal what they were unable to build in peace.

At first the United States considered itself blessedly immune from the world's violence and suffering. In 1914 President Woodrow Wilson urged unconditional neutrality as the way to safety during the European war. Neutrality was impossible; the United States joined the war and tipped the balance of opposing forces sufficiently to bring about the military defeat of Germany and an armistice in November 1918. Wilson then said that the unconditional acceptance by all nations of the ideals of altruism, democracy, and the League of Nations was the only way to secure lasting peace. The American people, however, denounced the League of Nations, and other countries felt that idealism was scant protection against the economic and political chaos of the time. By 1936 the League was dying, and the American Congress was busy passing laws designed to preserve absolute isolation when the next war, ominously visible on the horizon, swept over Europe.

War broke out in 1939 when Great Britain and France declared war on Germany for invading Poland. Germany and

1

Soviet Russia, in cynical collusion, divided Poland and the Baltic states. Hitler soon struck to the west. Italy, stabbing France in the back, joined her Nazi ally. In June 1940 France fell. Hitler dominated western Europe and was planning to invade Great Britain. In Asia Japan intensified her war against China, entered into formal anti-American alliance with Germany and Italy, and prepared to extend her conquests.

American public opinion changed before the spectacle of un-checked Nazi aggression. President Franklin D. Roosevelt won support for military and naval preparedness and material aid to Great Britain. The United States became the "arsenal of democracy." Congress put aside the neutrality laws and passed the lend-lease program in March 1941. Three months later Hitler attacked Russia. Americans forgot their dislike for the Soviet state and extended aid. Roosevelt claimed that his aim was to keep the United States out of war, but by late 1941 the Amer-ican people realized that the higher aim of checking Axis aggres-sion might soon make entry into war inevitable. On the Atlantic the American navy was skirmishing with German U-boats. In the Pacific Japan might strike at any moment against the tighten-ing web of American economic warfare. The blow came at Pearl Harbor, December 7, 1941. The United States was at war with Japan. Germany and Italy immediately declared war on the United States. The period of equivocal undeclared war was over.

Repeatedly and without success the United States had tried various unconditional approaches to peace and security: neutral-ity in 1914, idealism in 1918, isolation in the 1930's. Now the nation sought security by the unconditional defeat of the enemy. Since the enemy's existence was deemed the only significant cause of insecurity, men now assumed that a world consistent with American ideals and interests would emerge once the Axis powers were destroyed. Freed from enslavement and the fear of Axis aggression, all nations would embrace American ideals of democracy and peaceful conduct. If a misguided ally — Great Britain, for example — showed a tendency to stray from these ideals, a little friendly diplomatic persuasion would be sufficient to return her to the paths of righteousness. Absolute victory was achieved after four years and some effort had been made to change the behavior of allies, but Americans discovered in sorrow that peace was still unsecured. At the moment of victory in 1945 American leaders were on the verge of the realization that there were no unconditional solutions and that final, complete security in the twentieth century was unattainable.

The first diplomatic objective on the road to unconditional victory was coordination of the American, British, and Russian efforts. This was the task of the three heads of government: President Roosevelt, Prime Minister Winston S. Churchill, and Premier Josef V. Stalin. While the Big Three at the summit decided grand strategy and ambiguously discussed fundamental objectives of the war, their subordinates bargained to allocate materials, provide shipping, build bases, assign troops, and develop new weapons. The great decisions were tied to the outcome of the lesser and all required international negotiation. Diplomacy, instead of retiring to the sidelines until the fighting was over, became indispensable to every aspect of the war and thus to the life of the United States.

In December 1941 the potential power of the United States was great, but the immediate outlook was disastrous, far more disastrous than the American public realized. The navy was crippled; the army was an expanding swarm of civilians without sufficient equipment, training, or experienced officers; and industry was only partially converted from peacetime production. Germany controlled western Europe and her armies were wintering deep in Russia. Who dared predict that Russia could withstand the onslaught through another summer? Elsewhere German armies seemed on the verge of driving the British from Egypt and taking the vital Suez Canal. At any moment Franco in Spain might snatch Gibraltar. Hitler could then close the Mediterranean, dominate North Africa and the Middle East while choking the United Kingdom with a cordon of submarines in the Atlantic. The western hemisphere would be directly threatened. In Asia and the Pacific the only limit to Japan's wave of conquest was her own decision not to move beyond certain lines. Half of China, the Philippines, Indochina, Burma, Malaya, the Netherlands East Indies, and scores of smaller island groups were in her grasp. Would she seize India, Australia, Siberia, Hawaii? What could stop her? Anything was conceivable.

Fortunately, American diplomacy responded less to the immediate military peril, which might have been paralyzing, than to an optimistic view of the nation's historical experience and to the buoyantly confident personality of the commander-in-chief, Franklin D. Roosevelt. Americans later were to be led astray by too much optimism, but, on the dark morrow of Pearl Harbor, optimism enabled men to begin planning for victory. Notwithstanding the pain and humiliation of retreat in the Pacific, attention was turned first to coordinating strategy for the defeat of Germany. This priority was maintained on the sound assumption that Germany without Japan would be as strong as ever, whereas Japan without Germany could not long stand alone.

The remembered experience of the First World War exercised a profound effect on the diplomacy of European strategy. Americans had misleading and rather happy memories. In the summer of 1918 large numbers of American troops faced the enemy for the first time. By November the war was over. Admittedly, circumstances were now radically different, but the experience of 1918 combined with a natural optimism led Americans to favor a strategy of direct attack as soon as possible (preferably 1942 but certainly 1943) across the Channel on the center of German power.

The favored strategy of Great Britain, also based in large measure on experience of the First War, was totally different. From the autumn of 1914 until the summer of 1918, while the United States remained neutral or in a state of preparation, Great Britain and France had seen an entire generation of young manhood die in the stinking trenches of the western front. For four years gains and losses were measured in yards, casualties in millions. Now, twenty-five years later, France was conquered and Britain, having narrowly rescued her small army at Dunkirk, stood alone in Europe. What Englishman could advocate a deliberate return to the horrors of the continent before all other methods of attacking the enemy had been exhausted and victory assured? Certainly not Churchill, who had in the First War been a leading, if unsuccessful, critic of the stationary slaughter of the trenches. In the Second War Churchill, expressing his own and his nation's convictions, argued tirelessly against a premature frontal attack. By no means all of his alternative proposals were adopted, but he did succeed in postponing the main attack until Anglo-American strength was overwhelming. Until that attack came, in June 1944, the competition between the two strategies — the massive direct assault versus shifting operations on the periphery — was a central theme in Anglo-American diplomacy to which all other issues were in some way related.

Russia, the third great ally, had only one possible strategy: maximum defensive pressure against Germany while urging the United States and Great Britain to open the second front in Europe without delay and simultaneously hoping that Japan, a neutral in the Russo-German war, would not attack in Siberia. The keynote of Russian diplomacy was surly suspicion compounded from Marxist-Leninist-Stalinist theories, Russia's warped memory and interpretation of events since 1917, and anticapitalist propaganda which Soviet leaders no doubt had come themselves to believe. According to the Russian view, the capitalist nations had sought to strangle the Soviet Union at birth from 1917 to 1920, but having failed had sought in the 1930's to save their own necks by turning Hitler against Russia. Current Anglo-American friendliness was, in Soviet eyes, the product of fear and the mask to a continuing hope that Russia would bleed to death. Postponement of the second front in Europe was simply an expression of this hope.

British and American leaders were angered and hurt by the Soviet calumny, but they differed in their opinions of how to deal with it. The British were relatively unruffled and stoical. Russian suspicions were a fact of life to the British. Russian demands for an immediate second front were understandable, but must be firmly refused until the time was ripe. The idea that Russia might make a separate peace with Germany, as at Brest-Litovsk in 1918, if she did not receive full satisfaction from the West was dismissed by the British as nonsense. Similarly, the British argued that Russian cooperation or the lack of it in the postwar world would depend on the power structure at the time and not on fanciful Russian gratitude for favors which the West could not afford to grant.

The American attitude toward Russia was not monolithic, but the dominant view, to which President Roosevelt subscribed, was conciliatory, indulgent, and tinged with the vague fear that an unappeased Russia might make a separate peace. Roosevelt and his closest advisers were far readier than the British to meet Russian demands, to see an element of truth in Russian distortion of the past, and to insist that the way to win Russian trust was to begin by trusting, and making every possible allowance for Russian unpleasantness. Furthermore, Americans proclaimed time and again that the future peace of the world depended not on the balance of power but on the closest possible cooperation with Russia. That cooperation could and must be assured while the war was still in progress. In short, Americans were pessimistic concerning what Russia might do if her wishes were not met, but they were essentially optimistic in their belief that Western attitudes could shape Russian behavior both during and after the war. The ramifications of this Anglo-American-Soviet interplay appear everywhere in the diplomacy of the war. They affected the debate over grand strategy and they touched such questions as shipping and allocation of supplies. They lay behind the formulation of war aims for Europe, for Asia, and for the nature of the United Nations. In that interplay can be found some of the origins of the Cold War.

American optimism extended to the war against Japan. This segment of the conflict remained second priority until the day of victory in Europe, but it absorbed an increasing amount of diplomatic energy and military resources. The ocean war on the Pacific was an American show and required few diplomatic arrangements, but on the mainland of Asia diplomacy encountered its most complicated, difficult, and frustrating task: the support of China. Of all the allies of the United States, China excited the highest hopes and ultimately provided the most crushing disappointment. The reasons are embedded in both Chinese and American history as well as in the hard realities of geography and military power during the war. Had the China of

Chiang Kai-shek conformed to the romantic image cherished widely in the United States all would have been well. According to this image, which had flourished since the early nineteenth century, China was yearning and able to follow in the ways of its one benefactor and friend, the United States. If China could only be freed from the bondage of foreign oppression, an efficient, modern democracy would emerge. The Japanese occupation was a serious obstacle on this road to freedom, but, according to American illusion, the full moral support of the United States plus whatever equipment could be spared would bring ultimate triumph and a united, independent China, one of the four great powers (along with the United States, Russia, and Britain) upon whose permanent friendship the peace of the world would depend.

Such was the dream. Before long it became a nightmare. First, as in other areas of war, came the conflict of basic strategies. Naturally, Chiang Kai-shek considered that the center of the war was in China and that he should receive as much American support as he needed in order to preserve his position against the Communists and other domestic foes and then defeat the Japanese. For the United States, however, world strategy placed China fourth in line as a recipient of supplies: behind Anglo-American operations in Europe, behind Russia, and behind the naval war in the Pacific; and at no time was the United States willing to see its limited aid to China used for any purpose except the waging of war against Japan. Next came the problem of geography and logistics. Because Japan soon controlled all the land and water routes into China, every ton of supplies had to be transported first to northeastern India and then flown "over the Hump" at astronomical expense. For equal expenditure the United States could deliver hundreds of tons of supplies to England for every ton delivered in China. Last and most important was the relationship of the irreconcilable conflict between Chiang's government and the Communists. Few Americans could comprehend the murderous bitterness of this antagonism or why the Chinese could not forget their differences, like good Democrats and Republicans in the United States, in the patriotic struggle against Japan. Throughout the war and for more than a year afterward, it was American policy to seek to unify the Chinese factions. Seldom has an effort been so futile.

But in the days after Pearl Harbor none of these dismal facts about China was understood. Roosevelt, his advisers, and the American people looked forward to a triumphant partnership. Thus, in every quarter of the globe American diplomacy, sustained by an optimistic reading of the past and an unreal attitude toward the present, began its wartime tasks.

A factor that influenced the style and results of American wartime diplomacy as much as the nation's optimistic interpretation of the past was the personality of President Roosevelt. He took crucial diplomatic negotiations more completely into his own hands than any president before or since. One way to examine Roosevelt's qualities as a diplomat is to compare him with Woodrow Wilson. There was nothing cheerful about Wilson's solemn crusade of Christian good against the forces of evil. Roosevelt, in contrast, always gave the appearance of a happy man, sometimes to the point of an unbecoming and inappropriate frivolity. Wilson found it hard to like the individuals with whom he was forced to deal; Roosevelt's first instinct was to like everybody. Wilson was solitary; Roosevelt loved the crowd, huge parties, the feeling of presiding over a numerous family.

Associates found both Wilson and Roosevelt difficult to work with, but for different reasons. Wilson enjoyed admitting that he had a "one track mind." For long periods he would concentrate on a single issue and ignore others of equal importance. Roosevelt's mind, in contrast, was trackless. He would dabble in a dozen questions simultaneously and acquire a superficial acquaintance with thousands of details in which Wilson would have had no interest. Subordinates found it difficult to keep Roosevelt's mind focused for long on any one problem. He loved to ramble and he seldom studied deeply.

Wilson was stubborn and opinionated; his dislike for advice that did not conform with his own conclusions often became dislike for the adviser. Roosevelt, on the other hand, had a compulsion to be liked. In dealing with others he would feign agreement with an opinion rather than produce disappointment. In domestic politics this habit of trying to please everyone caused confusion but no lasting harm. When Roosevelt's final views on an issued emerged, the man who had been misled could resign. Many did.

But this Rooseveltian technique had doleful results when applied to international affairs, where all the favorable conditions that Roosevelt enjoyed at home were missing. Disagreements in domestic affairs were over means, not basic objectives. All Americans desired a healthy economy, an end to unemployment, and a broadening of security among the whole population. There were no disagreements that could not be faced and thrashed out by reasonable men of good will. But how different the conduct of international affairs, especially in the emergency conditions of a world war. The nations in uneasy coalition against the Axis disagreed not only on the means of winning the war, but also on fundamental objectives for the future. Differences were too profound to be dissolved by geniality, and disgruntled allies, unlike subordinates, could not be ignored. Roosevelt either forgot these truths, or else believed that his power to make friends was so irresistible that all opposition could be charmed out of existence. He was wrong.

There was another unfortunate connection between domestic politics and Roosevelt's diplomacy. As the most successful American politician of the century, Roosevelt had a superb sense of how much support he could command for his domestic programs. But in his understanding of what the people would accept in foreign affairs he was timid and unsure. Often he shied away from problems that needed to be confronted — Russian treatment of Poland, for example — because he feared that publicity might lose votes. He overestimated the strength of isolationism and underestimated the ability of the American people to absorb bad news and undertake new responsibility. As a result Roosevelt sometimes gave the public a falsely optimistic picture of our diplomacy, especially in regard to Russia and China. He also gave the Russians the impression that the United

States would probably withdraw into partial isolation after victory and that Russia, therefore, need not worry about American opposition to her postwar ambitions in Europe.

Two further traits of Roosevelt's character should be noted. The President had a small boy's delight in military and naval problems. Under the Constitution he was commander-in-chief of the armed forces and he set out to give practical as well as theoretical meaning to the title. Much of his time was spent in close consultation with military and naval authorities. Usually, he took the advice of the chiefs of staff, but on occasion he made important military decisions independently. Roosevelt's fascination with strategy and tactics intensified the American emphasis on military objectives to the neglect of those long-range political conditions to which military operations should always be subordinate. For example, in 1944 and 1945 Roosevelt concentrated so hard on the military objective of bringing Russia into the war against Japan that he seriously weakened American bargaining power in the settlement of permanent political objectives in Europe and Asia.

Finally, Roosevelt, unlike Wilson, was a pragmatist who lived in a world in which good and bad were somewhat mixed. He had no qualms about further blending the two, and for settling by way of compromise for the best that seemed available. Roosevelt was no metaphysician losing sleep by wondering if evil means could contaminate a worthy end. He was more inclined to act and let the historians worry about the philosophical problems involved in his behavior. The historian must conclude, however, that much of Roosevelt's diplomacy fails of justification even on its own terms. Too often the means were questionable and the results worse.

Roosevelt's character produced the worst results in his diplomacy with Stalin; with Churchill the best. Churchill and Roosevelt enjoyed the closest personal and official relationship that has ever existed between an American president and the head of another government. It was not, however, a relationship of equality. Roosevelt had the power and Churchill the ideas. Churchill, acutely aware of the British Empire's dependence on the United States, kept Roosevelt informed and entertained with an almost daily stream of imcomparably lucid and persuasive letters and telegrams. Frequently, he traveled to meet Roosevelt in Washington, at Hyde Park, or in Canada. Roosevelt never went to Churchill in Great Britain, although both Roosevelt and Churchill did meet Stalin on or near his home ground. Churchill's sincere liking for Roosevelt, his understanding of the President's character, and above all the range and penetration of his intellect served the British Empire and the Anglo-American cause well. No other man could have won Roosevelt's approval to such a large measure of British policy. But sometimes Roosevelt and his advisers did refuse Churchill's requests. On those occasions Churchill gave way with a grace that was as uncharacteristic of his past political behavior as it was serviceable for the preservation of the even tenor of Anglo-American relations.

Roosevelt's personal relations with Stalin were the least effective aspect of his diplomacy. The President met Stalin's displays of temper, suspicion, and churlish obstructionism with redoubled efforts at conciliation. Early in the war he tried to please Stalin by an implied promise of an immediate second front, and later he remained silent in the face of barbarous Soviet conduct in Poland. Sometimes he tried to win Stalin's confidence by ridiculing Churchill and hinting at a Soviet-American alignment against British colonialism. In personal relations and in diplomacy it is unwise and dangerous to pretend to denounce a proven friend in order to ingratiate oneself with a third party. Churchill bore the humiliation manfully; Stalin was not fooled. He listened to Roosevelt's chatter, said little himself, and coolly pushed the Soviet advantage in Europe and Asia without regard to the idealistic principles of political liberty to which Russia, as one of the United Nations, had subscribed. Stalin acted on the assumption, which Roosevelt's words and behavior amply confirmed, that the United States would raise no effective opposition to hostile Russian expansion. By the time Roosevelt's policy was reversed after the war, the Russian position had been consolidated, and the lines of the Cold War drawn.

The results of Roosevelt's personal diplomatic contact with the proud and haughty leaders who ranked just below the triumvirate, Chiang Kai-shek of China and Charles de Gaulle of France, were poor. Chiang and de Gaulle were similar in many ways. Each claimed to represent a great power suffering from temporary adversity; each was quick to resent the slightest reflection on his personal prestige or the sovereign prerogatives of his nation. Roosevelt, however, treated the two leaders in opposite fashion, acting more in terms of his preconceived notions about France and China than the actual situation. The President was an infatuated captive of the myth that China under Chiang Kai-shek was one of the world's great powers and deserved to be treated as such. He even toyed with the idea of giving Chiang a voice in the settlement of European affairs. No amount of evidence concerning Chiang's maladministration, the disunity of the country, the strength of the opposition, or the inefficiency of the Kuomintang armies appeared capable of shaking Roosevelt's illusion, at least until the closing months of the war.

For modern France, in contrast, Roosevelt had acquired an attitude of contempt as extreme as his admiration for China. He considered France a source of decay in the world, a politically and socially sick nation which by laying down before Hitler and giving way to the Japanese in Indochina had forfeited the right to be respected. Roosevelt saw de Gaulle as a pompous adventurer who represented only a clique of followers and who secretly intended to assume the dictatorship of his country after the liberation. Ultimately, Roosevelt's attitudes led to severe friction with France and to bitter misunderstandings on the part of the American people when Chiang Kai-shek collapsed so ignominiously in his civil war with the Communists.

Although wartime diplomacy, pervasively influenced by the personality of President Roosevelt, dealt principally with military operations, one overriding question was always present: what kind of world did each of the three major allies desire after the war? Each power sought, first of all, a victory that would prevent recurrence of a war as catastrophic as the one in which the world was then involved. American leaders gradually developed among themselves some broad ideas on how this might be done, but they believed that their objectives could best be achieved if specific discussions concerning the future were postponed until the fighting was over. Assuming that no postwar problem could be as important or difficult as the defeat of the Axis and that there would be time enough after victory to make detailed arrangements, they were insensitive to the way in which the conduct of war can prejudice the results.

From the American point of view, there were several ways that the goal of postwar security might be sought. Isolation had failed and was now discredited, more thoroughly than Roosevelt realized. A unilateral armed *Pax Americana* in which every threat to security was instantaneously smashed by the exercise of the superior force of the United States was technically worth considering, but was not politically or morally tolerable. A *Pax Anglo-Americana* in which the United States and Great Britian together ran the world had appeal for some Americans, and briefly for President Roosevelt, but it, too, was not feasible. Roosevelt until 1944 favored a peace secured by the armed co-operation of "the Four Policemen": the United States, Russia, China, and Great Britain — in that order of importance. Little countries would be required to keep quiet and take orders. This concept had numerous flaws. A power vacuum would be left in western Europe where, according to Roosevelt, neither Germany nor France would again be factors in world politics. This would be especially dangerous if Roosevelt's assumption of an identity of interest between Russia and the West proved unfounded. In Asia there was considerable doubt whether the Chiang Kai-shek regime in China could survive, much less serve as a policeman for others. In addition, the outcry of small nations at being herded about by the great powers would be too loud to ignore in the United States and Great Britain, countries which prided themselves on respecting the rights of others.

Churchill felt that Roosevelt intended to relegate Great Britain to a position of undeserved and unrealistic inferiority while encouraging the disintegration of the British Empire, a development which Churchill resisted with skill and energy. The Prime Minister's own program for securing the peace was equally objectionable to most Americans. Churchill, a strong believer in the traditional British reliance on the balance of power, assumed that the fate of Europe still determined the fate of the world;

that there was a basic conflict of interest between Russia and the West; that these differences should be faced openly and realistically; that western Europe had to be rehabilitated as quickly as possible with France and eventually Germany rejoining the continent's power structure; that the United States ought to cooperate with Britain in rebuilding Europe and be prepared, if necessary, to oppose Russian ambitions. Churchill believed that colonial peoples should receive increased self-government, but that the imperial powers should continue to exercise responsibility for their colonies in the interests of world stability.

Roosevelt abandoned the concept of "the Four Policemen" in favor not of Churchill's balance of power program but in response to the rising enthusiasm in the United States for the formation of a universal collective security organization, the United Nations. Secretary of State Cordell Hull, for example, argued that postwar antagonism between Russia and the West was unthinkable and that a third world war was the only conceivable alternative to full cooperation. Great power cooperation must be embedded in a world organization, a resurrection of the Wilsonian League of Nations. From 1944 onward Roosevelt and his advisers were fully committed to the early establishment of the United Nations as the only way to lasting peace. They became increasingly suspicious of Churchill's ideas. Ironically, many Americans came to believe that British imperialism and continued adherence to the idea of the balance of power were greater threats to security than anything Soviet Russia might do.

This does not mean that American leaders were hostile to Great Britain; rather they looked upon Britain as a misguided friend unfortunately wedded to dangerous and outmoded patterns of behavior. It was the duty of the United States to set this friend right for her own good and the good of the world. Russia, in contrast, was seen as the unfairly maligned giant, a bear too long harassed by an unsympathetic world. Russia had been so badly treated in the past that it was now necessary for the United States and Great Britain to make an extra effort to be warm and understanding. Roosevelt and many of his advisers believed that inwardly the Soviets yearned to be friends with the West, but were too scarred with unhappy memories to take the initiative. Russia's enormous loss of life in the war, approximately ten times Anglo-American losses, strongly reinforced the sympathetic American attitude. How callous it seemed to think ill of a nation that was suffering so horribly in what Americans thought of as the common cause of humanity against the barbaric Axis. In the face of this suffering, to treat Russia as a potential adversary, as the British were inclined to do, would perpetuate the atmosphere of suspicion.

While Roosevelt, Churchill, and their advisers privately wrestled with different theories for the maintenance of peace, the official public declaration of Anglo-American war aims remained the Atlantic Charter, a generalized statement drafted by the two leaders in August 1941, and subsequently accepted by all countries joining the war against the Axis. The Atlantic Charter denied that its adherents sought self-aggrandizement; it condemned territorial changes against the will of the peoples concerned, and favored self-government, liberal international trading arrangements, freedom from fear and want, and permanent security against aggression. Soviet Russia adhered to the Charter with the capacious qualification that "the practical application of these principles will necessarily adapt itself to the circumstances, needs, and historic peculiarities of particular countries." [1] In other words, Russia would not be deflected in the slightest by the Charter from the pursuit of her own aims in her own way.

Roosevelt thought that Russia wanted nothing but security from attack and that this could easily be granted. Personally uninterested in theory and President of a country where ideological passion was out of style, Roosevelt tended to assume that national security meant approximately the same thing in Moscow as it did in Washington. Unfortunately, even the Russians could not say where the line lay between the normal requirements of national security and the imperatives of Communist ideology. Russia's minimum territorial objectives in Europe were clearly

---

[1] Statement of September 24, 1941 by Soviet Ambassador to Great Britain Ivan Maisky, quoted by Herbert Feis, *Churchill, Roosevelt, Stalin: The War They Waged and the Peace They Sought* (Princeton, N. J.: Princeton University Press, 1957), p. 24. This and subsequent quotations from books by Herbert Feis used with the permission of Princeton University Press.

stated. They included restoration of the June 1941 boundary, which meant that Russia would enjoy the full fruits of the 1939 Nazi-Soviet pact, specifically the annexation of the three Baltic states, nearly half of prewar Poland, and pieces of Finland and Rumania. Germany was to be dismembered into a cluster of weak separate states and hunks of territory were to be given to Poland and Russia. Politically, Russia insisted on "friendly" governments along her central European borders. In practice this came to mean Communist regimes imposed by totalitarian means. In Asia the Soviets sought the expulsion of Japan from the mainland and the restoration of Russia's position as it existed at the height of Tsarist imperial power in 1904. This would entail serious limitations on Chinese sovereignty in Manchuria.

The United States shared these aims as far as they applied directly to Germany and Japan, but everything beyond that was in actual or potential conflict with the Atlantic Charter. By postponing decisions on these conflicts, Roosevelt convinced himself that he was preventing discord with Russia without making concessions that violated the Charter. But inwardly the President was quite prepared to concede these Russian aims on the assumption that once they were attained Russia would feel secure and would cooperate without reservations in the new world organization.

In retrospect it seems clear that Roosevelt's basic assumption was false. The evidence indicates that Soviet leaders believed that their state and ideology could never be secure as long as the world contained any large concentration of non-Communist power. Defensively they could assign no limits to the requirements of security; offensively they were under a compulsion rooted in Russian history as well as Communist ideology to expand the area of their domination wherever practical. Russian security and expansion were two sides of the same coin. A collective security organization was for the Russians an instrument to be joined or abandoned solely in terms of its usefulness in advancing Russian power in a world of irreconcilable conflict between capitalism and Communism; it was not the beneficent organization of universal cooperation envisioned by the more idealistic Americans.

Historically, most wars have been accompanied by considerable diplomatic contact between enemies; the two sides test each other's determination and bargain quietly over terms while the guns are still firing. In the Second World War, the war of unconditional surrender, the United States engaged in little diplomacy of this type. Germany and Japan, however, carried on negotiations within their spheres which significantly influenced the outcome of the war. To generalize, the Axis lost through blundering many of the advantages gained by force of arms. Had Germany and Japan been as skilled at dealing with each other, with neutrals, and with conquered peoples as they were in launching military offensives, the plight of the Allies would have been far more drastic than it was. Instead, Axis diplomacy was one of the greatest assets enjoyed by the Allies.

Hitler and the militarists of Japan came to power because the the German and Japanese people were dissatisfied with the conditions that prevailed after the First World War and found a totalitarian new order appealing. In like manner, Germany and Japan scored great initial military success because many of their adversaries lacked the will to take risks in defense of an international status quo which had not brought security, prosperity, or happiness. In order to exploit this advantage it was necessary for Germany and Japan to coordinate their activities and to convince the neutrals and the conquered that, as their propaganda claimed, the new orders for Europe and Asia offered genuine benefits for those willing to cooperate. They failed utterly on both counts.

In every war between coalitions one group seeks to drive wedges into the other. It was not necessary for the Allies to seek to separate Germany and Japan because they were never together, notwithstanding the alliance signed in September 1940. The two countries were profoundly suspicious of each other and withheld information with a fervor of secrecy more appropriate among enemies. The major, fateful decisions of each — Germany's invasion of Russia and Japan's attack on the United States — were made without informing the other in advance. Ultimately, these decisions meant defeat; perhaps it could not have been otherwise given the inferiority of the Axis in population and economic resources. But true coordination diplomatically arranged might have placed the outcome in doubt.

Geographical separation was, of course, a huge obstacle to coordination, but military action might have brought the two countries into contact. Far more divisive was ideological antipathy. Japanese propaganda stressed opposition to European imperialism and appealed to the idea of Asia for the Asians. It was thus most difficult to sympathize with the boundless growth of German power. Would Germany insist on acquiring new imperial status in the Far East? The Japanese could not be sure. Hitler's ideological dislike for the Japanese was even stronger. He was a believer in "the Yellow Peril" and found the spectacle of Japanese victories over white people most disturbing even when the whites were his enemies. In short, there was "a fundamental inconsistency in the alliance between Nazi Germany, the champion of the concept of Nordic racial superiority, and Japan, the self-appointed defender of Asia against Western imperialism." [2] In March 1942, to illustrate this point, Hitler is reported to have indulged in the thought that it would be satisfying to send England twenty divisions to help throw back the yellow horde.

Few countries have ever been as brutally and selfishly nationalistic as Germany and Japan during the Second World War. They went to war to satisfy that nationalism and lost partly because their nationalism prevented their cooperation. Still less could they cooperate with smaller countries and colonial peoples who had no love for the Allies and who might have been made into effective collaborators if the Axis had tried seduction instead of rape. In Europe Hitler had an opportunity of winning support from anti-Communists in the Balkans, Poland, and the Ukraine. But he imposed slavery where he might have made friends. He could have had far greater support from Vichy France and

---

[2] F. C. Jones et al., *The Far East, 1942–1946* (London: Oxford University Press, 1955), p. 102.

Franco's Spain if he had decided to offer them advantages in the new Europe. Different diplomacy and military strategy could have brought Hitler control of the Mediterranean and all of North Africa. He then might have exploited anti-British sentiment in the Middle East and brought that sparsely defended and crucial area into his orbit. India was also susceptible to anti-British appeals and if India fell, Germany and Japan would be united in control of the southern rim of Eurasia. This would have brought incalculable adversity to the Allies.

Similarly, in Asia Japan had great opportunities as she conquered colonies whose populations longed to be rid of European rule. By acting genuinely in tune with their propaganda and granting some scope to the national aspirations of these peoples, the Japanese might have forged a chain of allies across Southeast Asia. In many places they did receive a tentative welcome at first, but soon the arrogance and brutality of conquerors produced bitter hatred. The colonial peoples knew that European imperialism was bad, but Japanese imperialism was worse.

CHAPTER II

The Diplomacy of Counterattack

IN THE MONTHS after Pearl Harbor the Axis held the military
initiative. Defense and then counterattack were first orders
of the day for the United States. "We had to attack to win,"
wrote the general who was eventually to command all Allied
troops in western Europe.[1] The diplomat was servant to the
soldier, and the soldier dealing with allied counterparts served
as diplomat.

The news of Pearl Harbor filled Prime Minister Churchill with
a sense of exhilaration and somber thanksgiving: now eventual
victory was assured. He departed immediately on a battleship
for the United States with an entourage of high military officers
and economic planners. The conference in Washington which
followed (December 1941 and January 1942 — code name,
ARCADIA) reflected Churchill's high spirits and American optimism. On the economic level, for example, goals were announced
for the production of ships, on which all else depended, and
armaments. The figures were so incredibly high that many observers sniggered in disbelief. The goals were subsequently met
and surpassed thanks in part to the successful operation of a
variety of Anglo-American combined boards for the production
and allocation of resources.

The ARCADIA conference also succeeded on the level of personal relations. The President and the Prime Minister deepened
their rapport in formal daytime discussion and in private conversation over cocktails or late into the night at the White House

---

[1] Dwight D. Eisenhower, *Crusade in Europe* (Garden City, N. Y.: Doubleday, 1948), p. 26.

where Churchill was a guest. Harry Hopkins — Roosevelt's closest adviser and a man of energy, loyalty, ingenuity, and frail health — was always present to smooth over incipient disagreement. Hopkins was idea man, expediter, and legman extraordinary. In diplomacy his importance was second only to that of the President.

At the same time the generals and admirals were weighing each other's talents and personalities and creating an institution for unified command, the Combined Chiefs of Staff, which functioned successfully in Washington throughout the war. Some Englishmen resented the loss of status symbolized by the selection of Washington as headquarters for the overall direction of the war, but the tact of leaders on both sides prevented serious friction. Of particular importance was the mutual confidence and good sense of General George C. Marshall, the American chief of staff, and Field Marshal Sir John Dill, who remained in Washington as representative of the British chiefs of staff. The work of the Combined Chiefs of Staff was made easier by the decision of March 1942 to divide the world into spheres of primary responsibility roughly corresponding to each country's political interests. Responsibility for Europe was shared; the American sphere included the western hemisphere, the Pacific with Australia and China; and Britain had primary responsibility for Africa, the Middle East, India, and Southeast Asia. Later the United States felt compelled to encroach on the British sphere. The results, as we shall see, were always interesting and sometimes acrimonious.

The most publicized result of the conference was the reaffirmation of the idealistic war aims of the Atlantic Charter in the form of the Declaration of the United Nations, dated January 1, 1942. Drafted by the British and Americans, the Declaration was signed by all nations at war against Axis powers. Roosevelt chose the phrase "United Nations" in preference to the flat term "Associated Powers" which evoked unpleasant memories of disunity in the First World War. At the time men placed too much faith in the United Nations Declaration. Secretary of State Cordell Hull, for example, naively belived that the Declaration had made impossible a return to the secret bargains among victors which had plagued Woodrow Wilson.

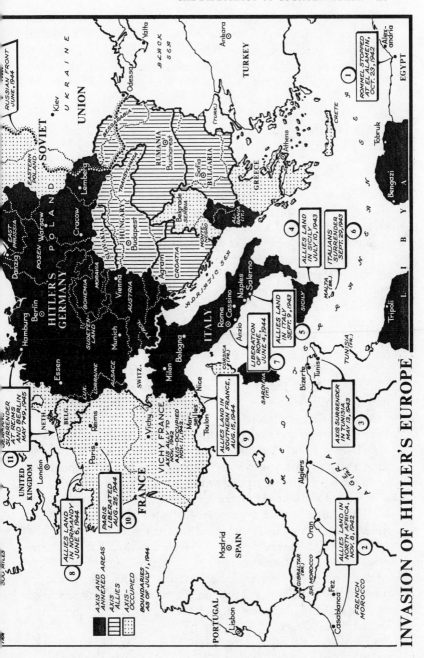

INVASION OF HITLER'S EUROPE

One lasting strategic decision was made at the conference: there would be no swerving from the informal 1941 Anglo-American agreement to remain on the defensive against Japan until Germany was beaten. The British had good reason to fear that after Pearl Harbor the United States might turn exclusively on Japan, leaving an exhausted Britain and Russia to stagger on alone against Hitler. Japan was the greater enemy to most Americans and the Pacific a more appropriate sphere for the United States than Europe. Dramatic voices like that of General Douglas MacArthur and stern ones like that of Admiral Ernest J. King were to be heard urging that more resources be allocated to the war against Japan. But the President was fully committed to the strategy of Germany first and so were General Marshall and his capable military planners. The temptation to make the defeat of Japan the first priority never disappeared, but it never prevailed.

The specific decisions of the conference were soon overturned by the misfortunes of war. In order to stop the Japanese and maintain a defensive area in Southeast Asia and the Pacific, the United States suggested and the British accepted the formation of a unified American-British-Dutch-Australian command under British General Sir Archibald Wavell. Before this command could begin full operation the Japanese had overrun the areas it was designed to protect: Burma, Malaya, Borneo, and the Netherlands East Indies. It became necessary in sheer desperation to rush far more ships, men, and supplies to the Pacific than had originally been intended.

The Japanese onslaught and the sickening success of the German U-boat in the Atlantic so depleted the number of available ships that the timetable for carrying the war to Hitler could not be followed. Churchill agreed with his military advisers that an attack on the continent of Europe was unthinkable in the foreseeable future. Instead he persuaded Roosevelt to favor Anglo-American landings in French North Africa with or without the approval of the French. Such an operation would take a little pressure off the Russians, clear the Germans out of all North Africa, and open vital sea lanes through the Mediterranean to the Middle East, Suez, and beyond. This operation was approved in January and discarded in February for lack of ships and enough trained men.

The euphoria of the ARCADIA conference soon disappeard. War news through the first months of 1942 was uniformly terrible. The area of Japanese conquest expanded without check. China grew more feeble. India was threatened. Australia feared invasion. In the Atlantic the U-boat was sinking many more ships than the Allies could build. As spring came on German armies resumed their grinding advance into Russia and the British defense of Egypt weakened. In Washington military planning, which had to be developed almost from scratch after Pearl Harbor, moved ahead. Dwight D. Eisenhower, working as an assistant chief of staff under Marshall, prepared a grand strategy whereby the British Isles would be used as the launching platform for an invasion of Hitler's Europe. General Marshall and Secretary of War Henry L. Stimson among others were convinced that this was the only strategy by which the United States and Britain could defeat Germany. Operations on the periphery, such as Churchill's project for French North Africa, would waste resources to no avail. Meanwhile Russia might go under. The army planners believed that a major cross-Channel invasion must be launched no later than the spring of 1943, but that a smaller emergency operation should be prepared for September 1942 in case Russia was on the verge of defeat. Great risks were acceptable to prevent such a catastrophe.

On April 1, 1942 President Roosevelt accepted the army plan and sent Hopkins and General Marshall to England to win British approval. "Dear Winston," Roosevelt wrote to Churchill,

> What Harry and Geo. Marshall will tell you all about has my heart and *mind* in it. Your people and mine demand the establishment of a front to draw off pressure on the Russians, and those peoples are wise enugh to see that the Russians are killing more Germans and destroying more equipment than you and I put together. Even if full success is not attained, the *big* objective will be.[2]

After a week of arduous discussion the British accepted the American strategy. Hopkins, who placed great emphasis on the necessity of helping Russia, was overjoyed. Marshall, with more

---

[2] Winston S. Churchill, *The Hinge of Fate* (Boston: Houghton Mifflin, 1950), p. 314. This and subsquent quotations from books by Winston S. Churchill used with the permission of Houghton Mifflin Company.

restraint, noted that British approval was carefully hedged with conditions. Colonel Albert C. Wedemeyer, a subordinate soon to rise to high command, suspected the British of duplicity, of accepting in principle what they never intended to carry out. British generals, in turn, privately belittled the military intellect of the Americans. Marshall was a gentleman, wrote the Chief of the Imperial General Staff, "but did not impress me with the ability of his brain." [3] The British were convinced that an invasion of Europe before 1944 would lead to disaster. An emergency operation to save Russia was even more absurd. If Russia was about to go down, they reasoned, it would be all the easier for Hitler to devour a landing in France.

In the weeks that followed, American planners became increasingly irritated with what they considered British procrastination and obstruction. Eisenhower and others went to England to build a fire under their allies, but returned discouraged. "It is necessary to get a punch behind the job or we'll never be ready by spring, 1943, to attack," Eisenhower noted. "We must get going." [4] At the same time Russia's apparently worsening plight convinced many Americans that the emergency landing in France had to be attempted, no matter how great the risk of disaster. The British, however, were less enthusiastic by the week. Their battle to defend Egypt was going badly. German submarines were preventing a build-up of force in the United Kingdom, and yet the public was clamoring that something be done to help Russia.

By June 1942 General Marshall, disgusted with lack of support from the British, was contemplating a radical reversal of American strategy, a turning away from Europe and a full effort against Japan. This would have pleased the American navy, but might have meant disaster for Britain and Russia. At this moment of crisis Churchill's thoughts ranged back to French North Africa and then to adventurous possibilities

---

[3] Arthur Bryant, The Turn of the Tide: A History of the War Years Based on the Diaries of Field-Marshal Lord Alanbrooke, Chief of the Imperial General Staff (Garden City, N. Y.: Doubleday, 1957), p. 290.

[4] Ray S. Cline, Washington Command Post: The Operations Division (Washington: U. S. Government Printing Office, 1951), p. 163. This is a volume in the official history of the United States Army in World War II.

throughout southern Europe. He returned to the United States to work on Roosevelt and Hopkins. The three men conferred first at Roosevelt's country home in Hyde Park, New York. Roosevelt was convinced by Churchill's persuasive unfolding of the advantages of landings in North Africa, but American military men from Marshall down believed that the operation (code name, TORCH) would mean an indefinite postponement of the main invasion of Europe (ROUNDUP, later called OVERLORD).

July was a busy month of military diplomacy in Washington and London. The British said they could not engage in an emergency landing in Europe in 1942. Marshall and Stimson argued against North Africa. Roosevelt decreed that American troops had to engage German troops somewhere in 1942. Since Europe was out, North Africa was the only alternative. Reluctantly but loyally the American chiefs of staff accepted the order of the President. General Eisenhower was named commander of the operation. Planning for the landings, which took place November 8, 1942, began immediately.

Thus, the basic decision was made by two men at the top. But in order to ensure the immediate and long-range success of the invasion, many tasks had to be completed or continued by diplomats at all levels on many continents. Beginning in the western hemisphere it was necessary to organize the twenty republics of Latin America for defense. Unless the security of the home hemisphere was maintained the United States could not devote the required men and resources safely to Europe and Asia.

This security could not be taken for granted. At worst the Latin American republics might split into pro- and anti-Axis blocs; their territory might become an unobstructed field of operations for spies, saboteurs, and political subversives; German submarines might find comfort in Latin American ports and receive directions from Latin American radios; the United States might be cut off from vital raw materials; and, finally, all hope of postwar unity in the hemisphere might be shattered.

At best all the Latin American republics might wholeheartedly join in the struggle against the Axis, take effective action with the United States to eradicate Axis influence from the hemisphere, and maintain an abundant flow of strategic material to the United States. The outcome was, fortunately, closer to the best than the worst possibility, but this result was not obtained without painstaking diplomacy on the part of the United States.

When the Japanese attacked at Pearl Harbor, the United States enjoyed strong assets but suffered under some liabilities in its relations with Latin America. The first asset was the Roosevelt "Good Neighbor" policy which since 1933 had convinced many Latin Americans that the United States had truly abandoned the "right" of intervention in the internal affairs of its neighbors. A second asset was the record of inter-American cooperation during the neutrality period of 1939–41. Several countries had joined the United States in specific deeds of hemispheric defense and all were on record in favor of unity against foreign threats. Caribbean, Central, and northern South American countries in particular believed that their security and the security of the United States were inseparable. Nine of these countries declared war on the Axis immediately after Pearl Harbor and three others broke diplomatic relations. Another asset was the American ability and desire to buy Latin American products at high prices while serving as the only large source of needed imports.

The greatest liability of the United States was the cultural and political resentment felt by many Latin Americans against the "colossus of the North." No amount of pious pronouncements in favor of good neighborhood could completely wash away that resentment. Latin American diplomats were extremely sensitive to American power and alleged domination. If the United States tried to persuade with too much vigor the strident cry of "Yankee imperialism" was likely to be heard. Another liability was the susceptibility of some Latin American leaders to aspects of fascist ideology combined with the presence in the southern half of the continent of a large Italian and German population. A final liability was American naval weakness at the beginning of the war. Chile with thousands of miles of Pacific coastline and Argentina on the Atlantic doubted that the United

States could protect them should Japan and Germany attack. Axis diplomats lost no opportunity to flaunt their strength and to emphasize the humiliation inflicted upon the United States at Pearl Harbor.

President Roosevelt exercised general supervision over Latin American policy but did not participate personally in negotiations, which for this region, unlike the rest of the world, were left in the hands of the State Department. The chief negotiator was Under Secretary of State Sumner Welles, suave, experienced diplomat, friend of Roosevelt and critic of Secretary of State Hull whom he considered "devoid not only of any knowledge of Latin-American history, but also of the language and culture of our American neighbors." [5] In January 1942 Welles headed the United States delegation to a conference of American states held at Rio de Janeiro in order to consider the emergency created by Pearl Harbor. The United States hoped to maintain hemispheric unity and obtain a declaration by all American republics that diplomatic relations with the Axis were severed. Before the conference opened Welles received assurances of support from all countries except Argentina and Chile.

The exceptions were crucial. Argentina and Chile ranked second and fourth in population among South American states, equally high in strategic and economic importance. If they adopted a strong anti-American line, as seemed quite possible, Bolivia, Paraguay, and Uruguay might swing into their orbit. At the conference Welles confronted the alternative of winning universal approval of a weak resolution which recommended that each country break relations with the Axis when circumstances permitted or forcing through a strong resolution which Argentina and Chile would reject. He chose the first alternative as the only way to preserve unity. Back in Washington Secretary Hull noted press reports that the United States had suffered a severe diplomatic defeat. In a fit of anger Hull ordered Welles by telephone to withdraw American approval of the resolution even though it had been passed by the conference. Welles was dismayed; he believed such action would destroy the conference,

---

[5] Sumner Welles, *Seven Decisions That Shaped History* (New York: Harper, 1951), p. 119. Quotation used by permission of Harper and Row.

encourage the formation of an anti-American bloc, and play directly into the hands of the Axis. In desperation he appealed over a three-way telephone hook-up to President Roosevelt who listened and then countermanded Hull's instructions. The resolution was allowed to stand as passed. This, wrote Welles later, was "the decision that saved New World unity." [6] Secretary Hull, however, remained convinced that Welles had blundered and that it would have been far better to defy than conciliate Argentina and Chile .The breach between the two men never healed. In August 1943 Hull forced Welles to resign from the Department.[7]

Reasonable progress was made during the remainder of 1942 in organizing Latin America for war. Chile, moaning about the Japanese naval threat to her coast, moved closer to the fold and finally declared war in January 1943. Argentina remained a problem far longer. From the sanctuary of her borders German agents transmitted information by radio, engaged in propaganda, and fomented unrest in neighboring countries. The United States applied a barrage of harsh words and some economic pressure. The situation seemed to be improving when the Argentine government broke diplomatic relations with the Axis in January 1944. But the government was shortly overthrown by a military coup d'etat engineered by officers sympathetic to Germany. The new government, nominally headed by General Edelmiro Farrell, but with Colonel Juan Peron as the dominant power, proceeded to establish the trappings of fascism in Argentina while defying the United States and giving comfort to Germany. To Hull this was intolerable. He began a campaign to smash the Farrell regime. Diplomatic recognition was withheld, punitive economic sanctions were imposed, Brazil was armed in preparation for war with Argentina, and Great Britain was

---

[6] *Ibid.*, Chap. 4.

[7] Hull gives his side in *The Memoirs of Cordell Hull*, Vol. 2 (New York: Macmillan, 1948), pp. 1143–1150. See also the documents in U. S. Department of State, *Foreign Relations of the United States, 1942*, Vol. 5 (Washington: U. S. Goverment Printing Office, 1962), pp. 6–47. Hereafter this important serial publication of diplomatic papers will be cited as *Foreign Relations* with appropriate year, volume, and special designation where necessary.

pressured into reducing ties with Buenos Aires. Hull's heavy-handed tactics served only to strengthen the Farrell regime and antagonize the British who depended on Argentina for nearly half their meat imports and who believed with good reason that Hull was exaggerating the extent of Argentine aid to the Axis. Until the end of his days Hull blamed sinister, commercial, reactionary, and British influences for thwarting him. In December 1944 he resigned, a physically and mentally exhausted man.

After Hull's resignation American policy toward Argentina rapidly became more conciliatory. In March 1945 Argentina declared war on the Axis in order to be on the band wagon of victory and receive an invitation to the San Francisco conference to establish the United Nations Organization. In April 1945 the United States extended diplomatic recognition and proceeded to override Soviet objections and secure for Argentina a seat at San Francisco. As victory neared, hemispheric unity seemed complete and peace in the western hemisphere permanently secure. Subsequent events revealed flaws in United States policy toward Latin America — especially the exaggeration of the external Axis threat and the related neglect of the region's vast internal problems — but in 1945 the outlook appeared optimistic.

The attitude of Spain, even more than that of Latin America, was crucial for the success of the North African invasion. Francisco Franco, the Spanish dictator, had risen to power during a bloody civil war (1936–1939) waged with military assistance from Germany and Italy. When the Second World War broke out Franco sympathized with the Axis but was determined to keep his exhausted country out of the fighting unless Hitler could offer an absolute guarantee of victory and enormous material advantages. Hitler's inability to make this guarantee was the reason Spain remained neutral. But a neutral Spain was still dangerous; thus, the need for careful diplomacy on the part of the United States and Great Britain.

Objectives were to prevent Spain from (1) joining the Axis as a belligerent, (2) giving military assistance short of going to war, (3) supplying the Axis with strategic materials, and (4) withholding strategic materials from the Allies. The first objective was fully achieved thanks to Hitler's failure, the second almost fully, and the last two partially. The principal method was economic coercion and concession. The United States preferred to inflict harsh treatment in the belief that Spain would behave if sufficiently injured by embargoes. The British placed a higher value on Spain's good will and argued that punishment should be infrequent and rewards generous. The actual treatment of Spain was a compromise: harsh at first but moving toward gentleness as the date of the North African invasion approached.

Had Spain joined the Axis she might have seized Gibraltar and closed the Mediterranean. By the time of Pearl Harbor, however, Nazi victory was sufficiently in doubt to make such a Spanish attack unlikely. But it was conceivable that Franco would allow a German army to cross Spanish soil. Economically, Spain was important as a major source of tungsten, a mineral essential to the armaments production of both sides. An advantage for the Allies was Spain's dependence on imports for petroleum, much food, and other essential commodities. Germany could not meet Spanish needs — the United States could.

When the United States entered the war it was decided in Washington to apply heavy pressure on Spain. All shipments to Spain, oil being the most important, were suspended on the double argument of scarcity in the United States and Spanish failure to meet American demands. The British and American representatives in Spain argued that this harsh policy was folly, that it was creating bitterness in the minds of Spaniards and paralysis in their economy. Resumption of shipments, on the other hand, would make it easier for Franco to resist German pressure and would increase Allied prestige. The State Department replied that shipments could not be resumed for their supposed political effect. From Madrid the American embassy warned of dire political, social, and military complications. A crisis was averted by Sumner Welles, acting during March 1942 as secretary of state in Hull's absence. Welles persuaded Roosevelt to order immediate oil shipments and also to appoint as ambassador to Spain the distinguished historian and eminent Roman Catholic, Carleton J. H. Hayes.

Hayes and the oil arrived in Spain in the spring of 1942; by summer there were signs of a Spanish shift toward greater cooperation. The tone of the press became less hostile, more favorable arrangements were reached in regard to strategic materials, and, most significantly, Serrano Suñer, Franco's brother-in-law and a violent Axis supporter, was replaced as foreign minister by General Gomez Jordana. "This means," wrote Ambassador Hayes to Roosevelt in September,

the replacement of a petty, intriguing, and very slippery politician, troubled with stomach-ulcers and delusions of grandeur, by a gentleman who is . . . honest, dependable, hard working, and endowed with good health and a sense of humor. To us, it means more — the replacement of a militantly pro-Axis man by a man who is pro-Spanish first and then more sympathetic with the Allies than with the Axis.[8]

Conciliation had succeeded. Three months later American troops landed in French North Africa and Spain watched in benevolent inaction. Thereafter, the United States and Great Britain had less and less to complain about as Hitler's star went down. By late 1944 the Spanish government was making overtures to the United States for special economic, political, and military understandings. Franco has ever been on the the side of the big battalions. The first diplomatic result of this new alignment came immediately after the defeat of Hitler. At the Potsdam conference in July 1945 Stalin said that Franco should be destroyed in order to make a clean sweep of the fascist dictators. Churchill defended Franco and cited Spain's helpfulness in the war. President Harry S. Truman agreed with Churchill. Stalin's proposal for the severance of diplomatic relations with Franco was defeated, although the Big Three did agree to oppose Spain's admission to the United Nations.

Spain's small neighbor Portugal was also neutral and also of great strategic and economic importance. Like Spain, Portugal possessed large quantities of tungsten vital to the manufacture

---

[8] *Foreign Relations, 1942*, Vol. 3 (1961), pp. 296–297.

of weapons. More important was her ownership of the Azores, mid-Atlantic islands which Britain and the United States considered essential as bases for the naval war against the U-boat and as way stations for trans-Atlantic air flights. Conversely, the Azores as bases for German submarines, rather than for their hunters, would result in injury to Allied shipping almost too great to bear. In 1940 Hitler had been on the verge of seizing the islands but had changed his mind when his naval advisers argued that the risks were too great.

Antonio Salazar, the Portuguese dictator, was not opposed to Hitler, but he performed as shrewdly as Franco in calculating his country's interests. Fearing that the United States and Britain might take the Azores by force (such an operation was under consideration in Washington and London from time to time), he used his limited bargaining power to the hilt. The United States generally allowed Britain, whose treaty relations with Portugal dated from 1373, to set policy, although Washington did try the tactic of having Brazil bring diplomatic pressure on her mother country. The British followed a policy of compromise and mild pressure, too mild in the opinion of many Americans, but with the improving military position of the Allies, Salazar began to do what he was asked. In 1943 he granted facilities in the Azores to Great Britain and to the United States in 1944. Meanwhile, the United States and Britain were paying high prices for Portuguese tungsten and threatening economic sanctions if Portugal did not cut off its exports of the mineral to Germany. In 1944 Salazar complied. Portugal thus moved, like Spain, from initial pro-Axis neutrality to a position of extending important aid to the Allies. The British decision, acquiesced in by the United States, to use subtle persuasion instead of a bludgeon on Portugal contributed significantly to this satisfactory result.

Some American idealists criticized their government for doing business with the undemocatic Franco regime and for being so gentle with the Portuguese dictatorship, but controversies over the Iberian countries were insignificant compared with the arguments that raged over American relations with Vichy France and Vichyite Frenchmen in North Africa. There were two sides to the French policy of the United States: the maintenance of diplomatic relations with the reactionaries and collaborationists who, from their capital at Vichy, administered the unoccupied portion of France after Germany's triumph in June 1940; and a concomitant, long-sustained antagonism to Charles de Gaulle and his anti-Vichy "Free French" movement with exile headquarters in London. When American troops invaded North Africa in November 1942, diplomatic relations with Vichy came to an end, but the United States continued to deal temporarily with Vichyite politicians in North Africa while ignoring de Gaulle. An originally loose and expedient policy had by the end of 1942 tightened into a knot of prejudice and misunderstanding which impeded our relations with France until the closing weeks of the war.

In the summer of 1940 Hitler, choosing to occupy only the north of France, allowed a nominally independent government at Vichy to administer the rest of the country and the French colonies. The Vichy regime was obnoxious to the American people, but prior to Pearl Harbor the maintenance of diplomatic relations did seem to have advantages. Hitler did not yet control the French fleet, French North Africa, or other strategically located colonies including those in the western hemisphere. By our diplomatic presence and occasional driblets of economic aid, we might encourage the Vichy regime to resist further concessions to Hitler. Also, our diplomats in France and North Africa might gather valuable information.

After Pearl Harbor, however, the Vichy policy came under violent attack. Liberals charged that the ideological purity of the American cause was befouled by contact with this fascist, puppet regime. Furthermore, there was no evidence that our recognition had inhibited the increasing subserviency of Vichy to Germany, nor was it clear what, if any, information our diplomats were gathering. Equally reprehensible, said the critics, was Washington's stubborn refusal to recognize Charles de Gaulle as a genuine representative of democratic France and a rallying point for the continuing struggle of patriotic Frenchmen against Nazi tyranny.

Any possibility that the American government might become more receptive to de Gaulle was destroyed in December 1941 by an affair of trivial proportions but with lasting and bitter repercussions: the St. Pierre and Miquelon incident. St. Pierre and Miquelon are tiny islands off the south coast of Newfoundland, anomalous remnants of France's eighteenth-century American empire. In 1941 the islands were under the jurisdiction of a Vichy official, Admiral Georges Robert, stationed at Martinique. The United States had made an agreement with Robert that there would be no change in the political status of French possessions in the New World. This agreement was designed to exclude Germany; it also excluded de Gaulle. When German submarines began to operate off North America, St. Pierre and Miquelon acquired sudden importance because of their powerful wireless station which could be used to communicate with submarines. In the midst of negotiations among the British, Canadian, and American governments for placing the wireless station under special controls, a small Gaullist naval force suddenly seized the islands. The American public cheered this swashbuckling and bloodless operation, but Secretary of State Hull was apoplectic with anger. It seemed that de Gaulle had betrayed his pledged word, and had proven himself an irresponsible and dangerous dictator; in the process the agreement with Admiral Robert had been violated. Hull issued a strong public denunciation of the seizure and received, in turn, an even stronger onslaught of criticism for his own anti-Gaullist prejudices. Having long enjoyed immunity from public attack, he was deeply hurt. His antipathy to de Gaulle became an obsession and continued to influence his behavior as long as he remained in office.

Meanwhile, the nature of the information received in Washington led to an underestimation of de Gaulle and an exaggerated belief in the utility of continued contact with Vichy. Admiral William D. Leahy, the American ambassador to Vichy until July 1942 and thereafter President Roosevelt's personal chief of staff, was familiar only with members of the Vichy government and had learned nothing of the undercurrents of resistance to Hitler which flowed so strongly through France and which ultimately rallied to de Gaulle. Similarly, the American agent in North

Africa, Robert D. Murphy, was in contact almost exclusively with conservatives who despised de Gaulle. Through no fault of his own, Murphy was incapable of judging what strength de Gaulle might be able to command. As the date for the North African landings approached, American planners believed that the only safe course open to the United States was continued cultivation of Vichyite elements who might be persuaded to join the fight against Hitler.

Thus, in the autumn of 1942 American agents tried to arrange with right-wing leaders in North Africa for the peaceful reception of American troops. This effort failed. American troops met sharp, although localized, French fire as they came ashore on November 8. It appeared that thousands of American and French lives would be lost. In haste a deal was arranged between Admiral Jean François Darlan, high-ranking Vichy cabinet member, and General Eisenhower as commander-in-chief of the American forces. Darlan ordered a cease fire and was obeyed by French troops. In return Darlan was granted political authority over French North Africa.

Although Darlan's precise political coloration is a matter of debate, he sympathized with some aspects of Nazism, was a violent Anglophobe, once would have been delighted to see a German victory. Now that the tide was turning, he saw a chance to save his skin. To the American and British public it appeared with some reason that the United States had installed a reptile who symbolized all that the democracies were fighting against. The protest was overwhelming. President Roosevelt, forced on the defensive, lamely called the Darlan deal "only a temporary expedient, justified only by the stress of battle." The public was not convinced. As an historian who was then an official in the State Department recalls, the episode "shook hard the faith of many in the durability of the principles for which we professed to be fighting, or in our devotion to them." [9]

Darlan's day, however, was short. He was assassinated on Christmas eve, 1942. General Henri Giraud, previously selected

[9] Herbert Feis, *Churchill, Roosevelt, Stalin: The War They Waged and the Peace They Sought* (Princeton, N. J.: Princeton University Press, 1957), p. 91. For a semiofficial justification of American policy toward the Vichy regime, see William L. Langer, *Our Vichy Gamble* (New York: Knopf, 1947).

by the United States to lead French troops in North Africa, was elevated to Darlan's place while retaining his military command. Giraud was a poor choice. Although an enthusiastic field commander with a romantic record of having escaped from German prisons in two wars, he was an incompetent administrator and a political child. Throughout 1943 and 1944 Giraud remained the American candidate to lead the French and resist the mounting influence of de Gaulle. But Giraud failed. After an interval of coleadership with de Gaulle, he slipped into oblivion.

At the time decision to invade North Africa was made, nearly every American military planner believed that the operation provided inadequate relief for Russia and was an unwarranted diversion from the main purpose of striking Hitler where he was strongest. They feared that the true continental front might be indefinitely postponed because of Mediterranean entanglements. Distant allies were even more disappointed and bitter. In Chungking Generalissimo Chiang Kai-shek was demanding that China be treated as an equal to Britain and Russia and be sent as many weapons and supplies. Ominously he hinted at withdrawing from the war by making a deal with the Japanese. And Stalin, beset by Hitler's full offensive power, demanded massive help from the western Allies. When the United States and Britain were unable or unwilling to oblige, he charged treachery and caused Americans to worry about the possibility of a separate Russian peace with Germany. The North African decision, in short, placed a heavy burden on diplomats whose duty it was to propitiate the disaffected and prevent the threatened disintegration of the coalition against the Axis.

CHAPTER III

Unconditional Surrender

JOSEF STALIN DEMANDED three things of his allies during 1942: formal recognition of Russia's territorial demands, enormous deliveries of military supplies, and a second front in western Europe. He was thrice refused. Chiang Kai-shek longed to see China become the center of the war against the Axis with his armies superbly equipped by the United States. He received less than Stalin. These denials were inevitable because of German and Japanese strength, limited Allied resources, the decision to undertake the North African invasion as the primary operation of 1942, and American adherence to the moral principles of the Atlantic Charter. Americans could not accept the inevitable with equanimity. They were haunted by imagined catastrophes that might occur if Russia and China were not satisfied. They sought to relieve their anxiety by explanations, promises, and then in January 1943 by the fateful announcement that "unconditional surrender" was the objective of the war against Germany, Italy, and Japan.

Russia, before the German invasion of June 22, 1941, was a semi-enemy of America and Britain. But Russia's valiant resistance to the full weight of Hitler's power transformed Anglo-American aversion to admiration by the time of Pearl Harbor. In the summer of 1941 Harry Hopkins, as Roosevelt's personal emissary, made a successful visit to Stalin in Moscow. Ever after

Hopkins and Roosevelt believed that personal contact with the Soviet premier could melt discord. As a material expression of the new American attitude, a lend-lease credit of one billion dollars was granted in the autumn and supplies were delivered as fast as ships could be found.

As the winter of 1941-1942 froze the German advance thirty miles from Moscow, the American and British governments were convinced that victory over the Axis would be in doubt if Russia left the war through defeat or negotiation with Hitler. This must not be allowed to happen. Beyond that one conviction, however, Washington and London mingled hopes, fears, and guesses to reach separate conclusions concerning what Russia might do in various circumstances. Separate conclusions led to sharp disagreement over the proper response to Stalin's three demands for territory, supplies, and an immediate second front.

Anglo-American disagreement over Russia was related to differing expectations concerning the nature of the postwar world. Americans looked for a radical break with the past; the British expected that continuity would be as evident as change and that past experience remained relevant as preparation for the future. Thus, Churchill and his advisers remembered that British security had for centuries been based partly on the existence of a balance of power in Europe. They reasoned during 1941 and 1942 that Russian friendship would be necessary to maintain that balance in the postwar world. Americans, on the other hand, wishfully thought that the old balance of power had been forever discredited. They believed the postwar world would be founded on benevolent international cooperation and scrupulous adherence to the ideals of the Atlantic Charter. The friendship of Russia was essential, but that friendship was to be achieved by destroying Hitler and thereby removing all threats to Russian security. It must never be sought by an immoral transfer of territory in violation of the Atlantic Charter.

Americans wanted very much to assume that Nazi aggression had somehow reformed and purified Soviet behavior. No longer would Communist Russia contemplate imperial expansion or political subversion in the interests of world revolution, at least not if the West showed that Russia had nothing to fear. The British were less sanguine. They believed that Russia would continue to expand against the wishes of the populations concerned, that nothing could prevent this expansion in eastern Europe, and that what could not be prevented might as well be openly sanctioned in the hope that Russia would not then seek for more. The British viewpoint on Russia, like the American, had elements of wishful thinking. The readiness to accept Soviet territorial demands was also a reflection of the British reluctance to take great risks in opening a second front in Europe. Americans, in contrast, hoped that a quick second front and ample supplies would so reassure Stalin that the territorial demands would be dropped.

The issue of how to respond to Russia became acute in the same week that the Japanese attacked Pearl Harbor. The British, disturbed by Soviet antagonism, sent Foreign Secretary Anthony Eden to Moscow in an effort to convince Stalin that Britain was not seeking a war of mutual German-Soviet exhaustion as the Russians appeared to suspect. In Washington Secretary of State Hull rightly feared that Eden might sign a treaty making territorial concessions in violation of the Atlantic Charter. He sent an emphatic warning. When Eden reported on the full extent of Soviet demands, Churchill — on board ship bound for the ARCADIA conference in the United States — used strong words which for the moment accorded with the American point of view:

Stalin's demand[s] about Finland, Baltic States, and Rumania are directly contrary to . . . Atlantic Charter, to which Stalin has subscribed. There can be no question whatever of our making such an agreement, secret or public, direct or implied, without prior agreement with the U.S. The time has not yet come to settle frontier questions, which can only be resolved at the Peace Conference when we have won the war.[1]

Eden accordingly told Stalin that a treaty on frontiers would have to be postponed.

Churchill's unwillingness to appease Stalin at the expense of principle was not shared by officials of the British Foreign Office or by the ambassador to Russia, Sir Stafford Cripps, a prominent Labor party politician and domestic opponent of Churchill. In

---

[1] Winston S. Churchill, *The Grand Alliance* (Boston: Houghton Mifflin, 1950), p. 630.

the following weeks Russian demands for a treaty grew increasingly shrill as did their complaints at the lack of a second front and the inadequate flow of supplies. Faint-hearted Englishmen, but not Churchill, began to believe Russia might make a deal with Germany. The approval of the American government was sought for territorial concessions.

The State Department reacted with angry indignation. Hull penned a long and fiery memorandum against a retreat from principle. He then fell ill and left Sumner Welles in charge of the Department for two months. On February 18, 1942 Welles had a verbal battle with Lord Halifax, the British ambassador. "Could it be conceivable that any healthy and lasting world order could be created," said Welles,

on a foundation which implied the utter ignoring of all of the principles of independence, liberty, and self-determination . . . in the Atlantic Charter? If that was the kind of world which we had to look forward to, I did not believe that the people of the United States would wish to be parties thereto.

Halifax, the attenuated aristocrat, replied with a patient disquisition on the necessity of using Russia as a counterweight to Germany after the war. Welles said such an idea showed "the worst phase of the spirit of Munich." [2]

President Roosevelt tried to postpone the issue by saying he would discuss the matter directly with Stalin, but the British would not be put off. The Foreign Office believed that Roosevelt was naive in thinking that Stalin would accept anything less than annexation of the three Baltic states — Latvia, Estonia, and Lithuania — on which the question of a treaty had come to focus. Sir Stafford Cripps, no longer ambassador to Russia, argued that Stalin considered the acceptance of his demands "the acid test." If they were met, said Cripps, Stalin would have no further desires; if refused there might result "a complete reversal of Stalin's attitude toward the war." [3] The British Cabi-

---

[2] U. S. Department of State, *Foreign Relations of the United States, 1942,* Vol. 3 (Washington: U. S. Government Printing Office, 1961), p. 520.
[3] *Ibid.,* p. 531.

net was frightened. Washington was told on March 30 that the British government would negotiate a treaty with or without American approval.

Here was the first major crisis of wartime diplomacy. Roosevelt weakened. He suggested that if a treaty must be signed there should be a provision allowing people "who desired not to be returned to Soviet domination to have the right to leave" their homelands. The President did not indicate where they might go. This, said Welles unconvincingly to Halifax, was "more nearly in accord with the spirit of the Atlantic Charter." [4] No one was happy with the concession. Assistant Secretary of State Adolf A. Berle, for example, touched the quick when he wrote to Welles:

I should have preferred (and I believe the Soviet Government would have preferred) a blunt and frank statement of our views, namely, full willingness to assure the satisfaction of every Russian interest consistent with the maintenance of the cultural and racial existence in their homelands of three free, decent, unambitious and hard-working peoples who are now apparently to be eliminated from the earth.[5]

Secretary of State Hull when he later reviewed Roosevelt's suggestion reacted in a similar fashion.

While the British prepared to negotiate a treaty with Russia, the Polish government-in-exile in London raised a loud and disturbing protest. Although the British did not intend at this time to make any concessions directly at Poland's expense, the Poles felt that a vital principle was at stake. Prime Minister Wladyslaw Sikorski said there would be incalculable consequences from the proposed abandonment of "a considerable part of Europe to Soviet Russia, whose final object is to provoke a World Revolution rather than subdue Germany." [6] The plight of the Poles was later to become the major issue between Russia and the West, but in 1942 Polish protests were regarded as an inconvenient nuisance. Many times the Poles were told to stop accentuating

---

[4] *Ibid.*, p. 538.
[5] *Ibid.*, p. 541.
[6] *Ibid.*, p. 141.

differences among the Allies and concentrate on the primary objective of winning the war. Sikorski and his colleagues, however, continued to mention unpleasant truths about Russian motives.

In April the Russian snow began to melt. Before long the German offensive would begin again. American planners entertained grave doubts whether Russia could survive without immediate relief in the form of a second front in Europe. To make matters worse the Germans launched an air, surface, and submarine campaign to stop the convoys carrying military supplies through the Arctic to Archangel and Murmansk. At this juncture General Marshall presented the grand strategic plan for a cross-Channel attack in 1943 with provision for the opening in 1942 of an emergency second front in France to avert a Russian collapse.

President Roosevelt, as we have seen, approved this plan on April 1, 1942. He quickly saw in it a solution to the vexing problem of Stalin's territorial demands. If the Russians could be persuaded that a second front would be opened without fail in 1942, perhaps they would desist from their embarrassing drive for a treaty in violation of the Atlanitc Charter. With tantalizing enthusiasm Roosevelt sent a message to Stalin:

I have in mind very important military proposal involving the utilization of our armed forces in a manner to relieve your critical western front . . . I wish you would consider sending Mr. Molotov [Soviet Foreign Minister] and a General upon whom you rely to Washington in the immediate future.[7]

Stalin cordially agreed, but insisted, against Roosevelt's desire, in having Molotov stop first in London for the negotiation of the controversial Anglo-Soviet treaty.

The sequence of visits was crucial. If Molotov got what he wanted in London, Roosevelt's scheme would be foiled. Accord-

---

[7] *Ibid.*, p. 543.

ingly, the Russian government was showered with sweet words about secret military plans and imminent improvement of the northern convoy situation. At the same time the British were subjected to more lectures on morality. Secretary Hull, up from his sickbed, cabled to London that if the treaty were signed it would be publicly denounced as immoral. "This would be a sharp break within the United Nations," Hull wrote later, "but there was no other course we could logically pursue." [8] Roosevelt in giving his approval to this threat blithely ignored the implicit commitment he had made to acquiesce in the treaty when he suggested the idea of transferring Baltic populations.

Molotov arrived in London, May 20, 1942, and entered into hard negotiations with Eden. The Soviet Foreign Minister refused to accept Roosevelt's suggestion about populations and then angered the British by making unacceptable demands concerning the Polish-Russian boundary and secret agreements directed against Finland and Rumania. Suddenly and characteristically when the talks were at their bleakest the Russians retreated, all smiles. On May 26 they signed an innocuous treaty which made no mention of frontiers but merely pledged the two countries to continue mutual aid in the war and not to enter into or conclude separate peace negotiations. "I was enormously relieved," said Hull.[9] Why did the Russians abandon an objective that they had been pursuing so insistently for nearly a year? Probably Molotov and Stalin decided that the chance of a second front in 1942 was worth a momentary political retreat.

Three days later Molotov arrived in Washington to collect payment for the concession. For nearly a week Molotov listened while Roosevelt talked. The President said he was glad that frontiers were not mentioned in the recent treaty, although the question could be raised at the proper time. On the second day Molotov came to the point. Was the United States going to establish a second front during the summer? "He requested a straight answer." As the interpreter recorded the conversation,

---

[8] Cordell Hull, *The Memoirs of Cordell Hull*, Vol. 2 (New York: Macmillan, 1948), p. 1172. This and subsequent quotations from the Hull *Memoirs* used with the permission of the Macmillan Company.
[9] *Ibid.*, p. 1174.

The President then put to General Marshall the query whether developments were clear enough so that we could say to Mr. Stalin that we are preparing a second front. "Yes," replied the General. The President then authorized Mr. Molotov to inform Mr. Stalin that we expect the formation of a second front this year.[10]

There was the promise, the implicit *quid pro quo* for the denial of the treaty on frontiers. After Molotov's return to Moscow a public communique was issued. "In the course of the conversations full understanding was reached with regard to the urgent tasks of creating a second front in Europe in 1942." it said.[11]

Roosevelt had purchased a few weeks of calm, but was courting more serious difficulty for the future because the promise could not be kept. Churchill tried to prepare the Russians for disappointment. They pretended not to hear. Inside Russia the press proclaimed that a solemn obligation had been given. The Russian people celebrated. On June 22 the American ambassador in Moscow warned "that if such a front does not materialize quickly and on a large scale, these people will be so deluded in their belief in our sincerity of purpose . . . that inestimable harm will be done. . . ." [12]

At that moment Churchill was in the United States persuading Roosevelt that a cross-Channel operation in 1942 was too risky and that the North African invasion ought to be undertaken instead. Meanwhile the Germans had sunk twenty-three of the thirty-four ships that sailed on June 28 from Iceland for Archangel. The British thereupon canceled further sailings for the summer. Within the space of two months Stalin had been denied all three of his demands. Roosevelt did not seem especially perturbed, but Churchill, fearing there would be hell to pay, decided to go to Moscow to explain in person to Stalin why there could be no second front in Europe. The confrontation with Stalin (August 12–16) was tempestuous. The Soviet dictator began by

---

[10] Robert E. Sherwood, *Roosevelt and Hopkins: An Intimate History* (New York: Harper, 1948), p. 563. This and subsequent quotations from Sherwood used with the permission of Harper and Row. For additional minutes of the Molotov-Roosevelt-Hopkins conversations, see *Foreign Relations, 1942*, Vol. 3, pp. 566–587.

[11] *Ibid.*, p. 594.

[12] *Ibid.*, p. 598.

accusing the British of cowardice in their attitude toward convoys and the second front. Churchill, for his part, repulsed Stalin's insults and unfolded the advantages of the North African and subsequent operations in the Mediterranean which he described as the "soft under-belly" of the Hitlerian crocodile. By 1943, Churchill said with assurance, the massive cross-Channel invasion would be launched against the beast's hard snout. Stalin's wrath was blunted.

In October it was Roosevelt's turn to worry. The convoy situation was little improved. German troops were at the outskirts of Stalingrad, on the great bend of the Volga, and the Soviet government was publicly blaming Russia's plight on lack of support from the United States and Britain. Stalin was relapsing into his normal attitude of distrust and recrimination. Suddenly the President saw "our whole relations with Russia" endangered. Ambassador William H. Standley was on his way back to Washington bearing an important message. Roosevelt feared it might have something to do wtih Russian withdrawal from the war. Words of reassurance were rushed to Stalin about convoys and possible air support for the beleaguered south Russian front. Then came the British victory at El Alamein in the Libyan desert followed immediately by the landings in French North Africa.

Roosevelt now decided that he could make an entirely new start with the Russians. He sent a colorful troubleshooter, Patrick J. Hurley, to Moscow without noticeable results. Next the President urged Stalin to come to a meeting with him and Churchill. Stalin said he could not leave Moscow, and Roosevelt settled for a meeting with Churchill and the Combined Chiefs of Staff, scheduled for January 1943 in Casablanca in French Morocco. Thus the year 1942 came to an end. The record contained little cause for encouragement, but Roosevelt, as he looked forward to Casablanca, felt his spirits rising.

By the time the United States entered the war, China had been fighting Japan spasmodically for a decade and continuously for four and a half years. The Japanese had annexed Manchuria in 1931–1932 and since 1937 had occupied the coastline and most of the major cities of China proper. That China still resisted was a tribute to the personality of Generalissimo Chiang Kai-shek. But by late 1941 it was doubtful how long this resistance could last without overwhelming outside aid. Chiang Kai-shek's government and party, the Kuomintang, were losing popular support and becoming increasingly incapable of coping with the country's rudimentary economy, political disunity, and premodern society. The bulk of the government's military resources were being husbanded as protection against internal Communist foes. Little remained to hold back the Japanese. The air was full of rumors of collapse or separate peace or both. Then came Pearl Harbor, a seeming gift from heaven. Chiang Kai-shek thought all his problems were solved. Unlimited American aid would pour into China. An immediate offensive under his masterful command would expel the Japanese.

Chiang Kai-shek's unrealistic hopes lasted a matter of days. Inside China nothing was done while everywhere the Japanese advance continued to mock the defensive plans of the western Allies. Hong Kong fell, then Malaya, Burma, the Netherlands East Indies, and the Philippines. China was cut off except for the perilous air route from India which itself was threatened. Meanwhile, the United States had made Britain a full military partner in the Combined Chief of Staff. Great quantities of aid were going to Russia. Australia had been saved, and a master strategy for Europe was being prepared. It seemed to Chiang Kai-shek that China had been forgotten. His outcries, loud and continuous, were heard in Washington where diplomats, military men, and economic experts tried to figure out what to do. Their desire was great, their achievements meager.

The situation was complicated by a highly emotional American bias in favor of the Chinese people. It was assumed that the United States had a unique mission to assist China and that the Chinese understood and were grateful. China, many believed, longed for nothing so much as American tutelage and help in expelling the selfish imperialists, among whom the Japanese were the most recent, who had denied China her rightful place. In short, Americans felt an attachment and responsibility for China which transcended the immediate object of victory over the Axis. If Churchill had understood this he would have been less amazed at "the extraordinary significance of China in American minds, even at the top, strangely out of proportion."

Churchill believed that the United States "accorded China an almost equal fighting power with the British Empire, and rated the Chinese armies . . . in the same breath as the armies of Russia." [13] In this he was partly wrong. Americans did play down the shabby reality of Chinese weakness. They *talked* as if China were a great power; action was another matter. It should also be pointed out that Anglo-American differences over China, unlike the differences over Russia, had slight influence on events. The British had little voice in Far Eastern affairs. They retained the habit of caustic comment, but left the decisions and responsibility to the United States. Diplomacy with China, therefore, depended largely on the interplay of internal American opinion.

There were three contrasting attitudes toward China held by American policy makers. The most extreme opinion, shared by many Far Eastern specialists in the State Department, saw the outcome of the war and the fate of the world depending on the American effort in China. The chief spokesman for this group was Stanley K. Hornbeck, who had devoted a long career to the thankless task of encouraging the Chinese to resist encroachment on their independence and to acquire the strength and skills of a modern self-reliant nation in friendly partnership with the United States. Hornbeck had been encouraged by China's fight against the Japanese and especially by the personal qualities of Chiang Kai-shek. His heart was so filled with high hopes for China that he paid slight attention to disagreeable reports concerning China's weakness. Daily he urged that the United States save China, win the war, and safeguard the future; daily he lamented what he considered the tragic and misguided strategy of concentrating on defeating Germany. In Hornbeck's opinion China was the most important issue in American foreign policy and any sacrifice elsewhere in the world was justified to meet China's need.

---

[13] Winston S. Churchill, *The Hinge of Fate* (Boston: Houghton Mifflin, 1950), p. 133.

The second group, which included President Roosevelt and several of his advisers in the White House, accepted Hornbeck's words about the importance of China and used them in propaganda for the public. Roosevelt's rhetoric, as Churchill discovered, placed China on a level with Russia and Britain. But the President's military decisions did not conform to his words. He made promises to Chiang Kai-shek but he never departed from the Germany-first strategy. Hornbeck, noting the gap between word and deed, thought that subordinates were sabotaging the President's intentions. It was not so.

The third attitude was held by American diplomatic personnel stationed in China. They had to deal with chaos as it was, not with comfortable theory. This group believed that China was a minor asset in the war against the Axis. The asset could become a major liability or with care could be slightly enhanced. The untruthful propaganda in the United States (sheer "rot," Ambassador Clarence E. Gauss called it) which depicted China as a great military power and Chiang Kai-shek as an incomparable leader was dangerous and should be stopped. The diplomats on the scene also considered that the inefficiency and corruption of Chiang Kai-shek's regime were as great an obstacle to progress as the Japanese. They urged reform. Most American military men in China also believed that China's war-making potential was exaggerated in Washington, but that the situation could be improved by internal Chinese reforms.

Immediately after Pearl Harbor Generalissimo Chiang Kaishek asked for a China-first strategy. In reply he was named commander of Allied forces in China, without the forces except his own ill-trained armies and a token unit of American airmen. Soon he asked for full Chinese representation on the Combined Chiefs of Staff and on the board that allocated available weapons among the Allies. He was refused then and every time he made the same request throughout the war. He asked for more lend-lease equipment; but the British took for the defense of Burma a quantity of lend-lease material en route to China. He asked for men, planes, trucks, and guns. There was little to spare and no ships in which to carry it.

He also asked for money — $500,000,000 from the United States and a like amount from Great Britain. The British said no, but the Americans, frustrated by their inability to give concrete aid and obsessed by the fear that China would leave the war, eagerly embraced the idea. From Chungking an agent of the U. S. Treasury wrote, "a substantial loan to China, the bigger the better, would be invaluable in keeping China going against the Axis." [14] Others said it would bolster Chiang's regime. The money would be a token of American faith in China and might be used to check inflation, but as long as transportation was lacking there was nothing it could buy. Ambassador Gauss admitted a smaller loan might have a useful political impact but, fearing personal profiteering and corruption among the recipients, he said the United Statts should have some assurance that the money was put to good use. The Chinese government said it would regard any strings attached to the loan as an insult. The officials in Washington agreed: half a billion and no strings. As Herbert Feis, who participated in the negotiations, has written:

The President's compliance was due in part to the compulsion he felt to evade Chinese requests to share in the making of decisions about the distribution of weapons among the various Allies. General Marshall urged quick action, since he thought that the fall of Singapore and Rangoon might give great force to the Japanese appeal to the races of Asia to stand together. Stimson agreed, believing that we must at any price keep China in the war.[15]

On February 6, 1942 Congress passed the necessary appropriation without a dissenting vote.

The money soon disappeared, as Gauss feared, into obscure places. Inflation continued unchecked, as did talk of "undeclared peace" between China and Japan, and the Generalissimo's complaints. "China is treated not as an equal like Britain and Russia, but as a ward," he said in April for Roosevelt's notice.[16] Meanwhile, a hard-nosed American general with experience in China and a knowledge of the language, Joseph W. Stilwell, arrived in China to head the American military effort and to serve as Chiang's chief of staff. Chiang and Stilwell quickly

---

[14] *Foreign Relations, 1942, China* (1956), p. 419.

[15] Herbert Feis, *The China Tangle* (Princeton, N. J.: Princeton University Press, 1953), p. 22.

[16] *Foreign Relations, 1942, China*, p. 33.

developed a violent personal antipathy which grew stronger as the American's efforts to reform the Chinese armies and infuse some fighting spirit came to naught. Stilwell would have been recalled except that General Marshall considered him the best man for the job.

In June 1942 British setbacks in North Africa led to the diversion of bombers and transport planes from China to the Middle East. Cargo deliveries into China suffered. "Now what can I say to the G-mo?" General Stilwell wrote in his diary. "We fail in *all* our commitments, and blithely tell him to just carry on, old top." [17] Chiang asked Roosevelt to send Harry Hopkins to Chungking, but a lesser White House aide went out instead. By mid-summer, when the decision to concentrate on the North African invasion was made, American attitudes toward China were in a state of confusion. The embassy in Chungking believed that little could be done without internal reform. One diplomat reported that the National government sought "to insure its own perpetuation and domestic supremacy and to come to the peace table as militarily powerful as possible." The United States could not "induce the Chinese to assume the offensive" unless Chiang believed that all equipment used "will be immediately replaced with interest." [18] But in the State Department, Hornbeck was crying out,

China can be kept in this war at a comparatively small cost. China can be made a base of operations from which Japan can be greatly damaged, at a comparatively small cost. China and the whole Far East can be lost as effective allies and, if lost, can be turned against the Occident. . . . [19]

Subordinates argued, but Roosevelt and the American chiefs of staff went on planning grand strategy for Europe. They neglected China but felt they had no choice.

At this point Secretary of State Hull, hovering ineffectually on the edges of China policy, decided on a special gesture: the relinquishment by the United States and Great Britain of extra-

---

[17] Quoted by Feis, *The China Tangle*, p. 43.

[18] Memorandum by John P. Davies, July 31, 1942, *Foreign Relations, 1942, China*, p. 129.

[19] Memorandum by Stanley K. Hornbeck, August 17, 1942, *ibid.*, p. 139.

territorial rights. For a century Western nations had enjoyed special privileges in China including the right to have their citizens tried by western, not Chinese, courts for crimes committed in China. This was the right of "extraterritoriality." Hull reasoned that a voluntary abandonment of this right and other privileges would encourage the faltering Chinese war effort. The British questioned the timing of the gesture and suggested that it might be received cynically since the Japanese occupied most of the areas where the privileges had been enjoyed. Ambassador Gauss warned Hull not to expect any gratitude from the Chinese. Hull, however, was enthusiastic; he argued that American public opinion demanded this act of generosity. The British agreed to go along. A treaty abandoning all special rights was negotiated and formally signed January 11, 1943. This gesture, like the half-billion-dollar loan, had no discernible effect.

The months went by and the sense of crisis continued. President Roosevelt tried a little personal charm. On the eve of the Casablanca confeernce he tempted Chiang with visions of China's great future as one of the "Four Policemen" and as the leader in the abolition of colonialism in Asia. Chiang appeared not to be impressed and instead felt resentment that he had not been invited to Casablanca. Roosevelt, however, hoped that a new approach might emerge from that conference with Churchill. On January 9, 1943 he left Washington on the first of his three momentous overseas missions.

Roosevelt was accompanied by Harry Hopkins and the American chiefs of staff, but he deliberately excluded Secretary of State Hull. (Churchill wanted to bring Foreign Secretary Eden, but Roosevelt said no: if Eden comes it will be hard to keep Hull away.) This decision reflected the declining importance of the State Department in the formulation of wartime foreign policy. It was also indicative of the President's jaunty overconfidence in his ability to make great decisions with little preparation and without systematic advice. From Casablanca until his death the President took diplomacy more and more into his own hands at a time when his health, memory, and powers of concentration were declining.

The tone of the Casablanca conference was buoyant. The tide of battle was turning. All of Africa would soon be in Allied hands, although not quite as soon as expected. The Russians were winning a great victory at Stalingrad and ever after would grow stronger while the German armies retreated. On the Pacific the American navy had gained ascendancy over the Japanese. Soon the island-hopping advance toward Tokyo would begin. Only in China was the prospect grimmer than on the day of Pearl Harbor. Roosevelt and Churchill accordingly enjoyed the warm Moroccan sunshine, good food and drink, and a chance to relax. Through most of the conference disturbing thoughts of Russia and China did not intrude.

The chief military purpose of Casablanca was to decide what to do next. Against General Marshall's better judgment, the invasion of Sicily was approved. Marshall feared another diversion, sucking resources and stealing time from the major cross-Channel attack. He wanted to put an end to "periphery pecking" once and for all. But the British argued successfully that an attack on Sicily might knock Italy out of the war and was the best way to use the troops and men then in North Africa pending the time when the big attack was ready. The basic strategy, however, was reaffirmed and planning for the cross-Channel invasion (soon to be called OVERLORD) was accelerated. In May 1942 Roosevelt had promised this second front for 1942; in Moscow in August Churchill had promised it for 1943; now 1944 was established as the most likely target date. The Russians would not be happy when they learned. It was also decided to increase the weight of the strategic bombing offensive against Germany, to continue to send supplies to Russia, and to let the Americans step up operations in the Pacific. But China got short shrift. A campaign to recapture Burma in 1943 was tentatively approved (but quickly postponed after the conference) and the combat and transport air effort in China was to be increased slightly.

From the military point of view Casablanca marked a turning point. The phase of defense and first desperate counterattack was over. The basic decisions had been made. Victory was far off, but in sight. For the political leaders the time had come to indicate something of the terms of that victory. What would happen to enemies? Even more important, what would happen to allies? These were most difficult questions to which Roosevelt preferred to give as little thought as possible. But at Casablanca he realized that there were great dangers lurking in a policy of total silence, and great advantages in proclaiming that the United States would fight until the unconditional surrender of the Axis was achieved.

The danger of continued silence was the possibility that Russia and China might become so distrustful of Anglo-American motives that they would precipitate the break-up of the great coalition on the threshold of victory. What then would happen to the stability of the postwar world? Roosevelt in particular placed great emphasis on the long-term cooperation of the "Four Policemen." Unfortunately, the record of events during 1942 did not of itself give much ground for optimism. Stalin had been denied all three basic demands and, so the Soviets charged, had been deceived in the bargain. China had been told to carry on, but had received very little concrete assistance. Both Stalin and Chiang Kai-shek were continually implying or charging the West with bad faith and nefarious motives. The Generalissimo asked if Asians were always to be treated as inferiors. "If we are thus treated during the stress of war, what becomes of our position at the peace conference?" [20] The Soviets in their turn seemed wedded to the dark suspicion that Britain and the United States desired Russia to suffer maximum injury and to emerge from the war as weakened as Germany, thus leaving the world for the capitalists. The recent dealing with the late unlamented Vichyite Admiral Darlan had served to increase the climate of suspicion. Inevitably the question arose whether the United States and Britain might not connive in similar fashion with Hitler or Japan at the expense of Russia and China.

Unless something was said at Casablanca to remove these ominous Russian and Chinese thoughts, the conference could not be considered a success. Roosevelt's hope for a clean start on relations with these two difficult allies would be tragically dis-

---

[20] *Ibid.*, p. 34.

appointed. An authoritative guarantee was needed that the United States and Britain would not lay down their arms before the objectives of all four Allies *vis-à-vis* the Axis were achieved. But Roosevelt could not give a description of specific objectives lest they interfere with the Atlantic Charter. Also, everyone remembered the difficulties Woodrow Wilson had encountered with his "Fourteen Points." None of the victors of 1918 had been satisfied and, what was worse, Germany had charged that she had been tricked into an armistice on the basis of conditions that were then violated. Planners in the State Department suggested to Roosevelt that this time the enemy must have no chance to claim that he was not completely defeated. Roosevelt liked the suggestion.

Roosevelt decided before leaving Washington for Casablanca that he would announce the demand of unconditional surrender. The phrase was discussed in a desultory fashion at the conference with Churchill, but then laid aside for other matters including the planning of specific military operations and a comic opera interlude when Roosevelt and de Gaulle met for the first time and formed mutually unpleasant impressions. But on the last day of the meeting Roosevelt spoke to a press conference.

Peace can come to the world only by the total elimination of German and Japanese war power. . . . The elimination of German, Japanese, and Italian war power means the unconditional surrender by Germany, Italy, and Japan. That means a reasonable assurance of future world peace. It does not mean the destruction of the population of Germany, Italy, or Japan, but it does mean the destruction of the philosophies in those countries which are based on conquest and the subjugation of other people.[21]

Churchill, who had forgotten about the unconditional surrender formula, associated Great Britain unequivocally with the proclamation. The two leaders sent hearty messages to Stalin and Chiang Kai-shek and the conference came to an end. The future would reveal whether unconditional surrender would have the marvelous effect on Russia and China which Roosevelt hoped.

---

[21] Quoted by Herbert Feis, *Churchill, Roosevelt, Stalin: The War They Waged and the Peace They Sought* (Princeton, N. J.: Princeton University Press, 1957), p. 109.

The proclamation of unconditional surrender has been condemned by scores of writers as one of the great mistakes of the war. Critics argue that the war was unnecessarily prolonged at terrible cost because the German and Japanese people believed that unconditional surrender would mean individual and national annihilation. Therefore, they fought on with the fanatical desperation of the doomed. These critics conveniently play down the fact that the original proclamation, supplemented by many public statements by Roosevelt and Churchill, indicated that unconditional surrender did not mean extermination or mass slavery for the defeated. Guilty governments were to be eliminated unconditionally, but peoples would be rehabilitated and in time normal national life might be resumed. It is true that German and Japanese propagandists distorted the phrase in order to maintain the war spirit of the people, but propagandists can distort anything for such purposes. It is also true that after Hitler's defeat many German leaders claimed that the Führer would have been overthrown except for the demoralizing impact of the unconditional surrender formula on the anti-Nazi resistance. Such testimony, however, must be used with extreme caution for it comes from those who sought in defeat to give the impression that they had opposed Hitler always and thus did not share the guilt of Hitler's atrocities. The charge that unconditional surrender prolonged Japan's will to fight is less substantial and applies primarily to the American refusal to promise that Japan could keep the institution of Emperor.

What then was the harm of unconditional surrender? The harm was in the impact of the slogan on the formulation of American policy. Unconditional surrender was in spirit the antithesis of careful long-range planning. It encouraged the delusion that once the Axis was defeated there would be few obstacles in the way of establishing the wonderful world of peace. Unconditional surrender woud wipe the slate clean. Sporadically, some Americans, nevertheless, did attempt to plan, but their efforts were disconnected, on a small scale, unsustained at the highest level, and never coordinated into a unified policy. Unconditional surrender and the practice of postponing all issues not directly connected with defeating the Axis were complementary aspects of the same attitude.

CHAPTER IV

Optimism at Teheran, 1943

PRESIDENT ROOSEVELT, with his personal influence over American diplomacy at its peak, was pleased with the results of the year 1943. Italy surrendered; China was recognized in principle as one of the four great powers; and Anglo-American differences over strategy were blended into a firm decision to launch the cross-Channel invasion in the spring of 1944. Russia responded with a public pledge to support a postwar world security organization and indicated secretly that she would enter the war against Japan after Germany's defeat. The year ended in a climax of apparent good will and unity at Teheran when Roosevelt, Churchill, and Stalin met together for the first time.

Optimism nourished by military success could not have been maintained without a faith in Russia's willingness to cooperate in the postwar world. Holding to that faith, American leaders in 1943 believed it was wise to explore the political issues which would have to be solved after the defeat of the Axis while postponing all difficult decisions on the assumption that victory would make the thorniest problem seem easy. They also assumed that the United States would withdraw quickly from direct involvement in European affairs after the war; thus, they believed that military decisions should be designed to defeat the enemy as quickly as possible and to minimize the chance of future political commitments. They had little awareness that the events and attitudes of 1943 would narrow the range of alternatives which remained open when the political decisions of 1945 were made.

After the Casablanca conference in January, General Marshall and his colleagues on the American Joint Chiefs of Staff worried that the peripheral operations which began with the North African invasion might delay indefinitely the decisive cross-Channel attack. At Casablanca the British prevailed with arguments in favor of an attack on Sicily as the next step. "We came, we listened and we were conquered," General Marshall's chief adviser on strategy commented bitterly.[1] The gloomy planners asked what next: the Italian mainland, Aegean islands, the Balkans? Would diversions never end?

The arrival of spring brought a welcome change in outlook. President Roosevelt, who had overruled the Joint Chiefs by deciding on the North African invasion in 1942, now became less interested in Churchill's peripheral strategy and started to give more support to his own military advisers. The shift was partly the result of the growing influence of Admiral William D. Leahy who, as personal chief of staff to Roosevelt and chairman of the Joint Chiefs, interpreted each to the other. He believed passionately in the cross-Channel operation, was deeply antagonistic to British suggestions, and retained many isolationist assumptions concerning America's future role in European affairs. Leahy did not shape policy directly, but by controlling much of the military information that reached the President's desk he conditioned the atmosphere in which decisions were made.

The change was evident at TRIDENT, the full-dress diplomatic and military conference held with the British in Washington in May 1943. With the President's support, Marshall won agreement to the principle that further Mediterranean operations would be undertaken only if they did not constitute a drain on the build-up for the main attack in 1944. The Americans, in turn, agreed that the elimination of Italy from the war was a practical

---

[1] General Albert C. Wedemeyer quoted by Ray S. Cline, *Washington Command Post: The Operations Division* (Washington: U. S. Government Printing Office, 1951), p. 236.

objective for 1943 and the British for the first time accepted a precise target date for the cross-Channel attack: May 1, 1944. At the same time an increase in the tempo of Pacific operations was sanctioned. Only in China did the military situation remain unimproved.

In the summer Americans completed basic plans for the great operation, now known as OVERLORD, and secured further British commitment at the QUADRANT conference in Quebec during August. Meanwhile, Mussolini had been ousted as head of the Italian government (July 25, 1943) and his successor, Marshal Pietro Badoglio, was hinting at Italy's readiness to switch sides. In August Sicily fell into Anglo-American hands and during the first days of September the Italian government surrendered as Allied troops landed on the mainland. By now the tide was running strongly against Germany in Russia. The Red Army, after the crucial victory at Stalingrad in January 1943, gained the permanent initiative. Stalin gradually became convinced that the cross-Channel invasion would, at least, take place as promised. At Teheran he smiled. The last vestige of fundamental Anglo-American strategic uncertainty for Europe was removed in December at the SEXTANT conference in Cairo. An official military historian has written: "If, in planning for the offensive phase of coalition warfare against Germany, TRIDENT symbolized for American strategists a half-way mark, and QUADRANT the start of the final lap, SEXTANT represented the reaching of the goal." [2] There were still military disagreements in the months ahead, but they dealt with tactics and political implications rather than with grand strategy.

That, in brief, was the optimistic background to the year's political discussions. The British, convinced of the necessity of making political plans, took the initiative by sending Foreign Secretary Eden to Washington in March 1943. The significant portion of the Eden conversations took place in the White House with Roosevelt and Harry Hopkins, who filled the role of Secretary of State while unhappy Hull, the real Secretary, was pushed

---

[2] Maurice Matloff, *Strategic Planning for Coalition Warfare, 1943–1944* (Washington: U. S. Government Printing Office, 1959), p. 383. This is a volume in the official history of the *United States Army in World War II*.

farther into obscurity. The President's habit of excluding Hull from all important conversations meant that the professional officers of the State Department were isolated from the conduct of foreign policy. They worked hard, wrote detailed and often discerning memoranda, and made recommendations, but the President seldom acknowledged their existence.

Russia was the first topic in the White House talks with the British Foreign Secretary. Roosevelt asked Eden for an opinion on the thesis "that the Soviet Government was determined to dominate all of Europe by force of arms or by force of communist propaganda." Eden replied with an optimistic analysis which the British later abandoned. Stalin, he said, hoped for cooperation with the United States and Britain but "in any event a wise and expedient thing was to cultivate to the utmost . . . the friendship and confidence of the Soviet Government." Roosevelt agreed wholeheartedly. The conversation turned to Russia's territorial objectives. Eden said Stalin would insist on permanent annexation of the three Baltic states. Roosevelt answered that this was lamentable but also unpreventable. He hoped for the sake of appearances that Russia would conduct new plebiscites to show that the Baltic people wanted to be incorporated into the U. S. S. R. Next came some discussion of the friction between Russia and the Polish government-in-exile. It was agreed that the London Poles were troublemakers whose complaints and unreasonable demands were endangering relations with Russia. Roosevelt said that a Polish settlement would have to be dictated; "as far as Poland is concerned, the important thing is to set it up in a way that will maintain the peace of he world." This readiness to dictate to a small power reflected Roosevelt's conviction that the "Four Policemen" would run the world. He said there might be a world organization with general membership, "but . . . the real decisions should be made by the United States, Great Britain, Russia and China, who would . . . have to police the world." The President laid particular emphasis on the importance of strengthening China as the leading power in Asia. Eden disagreed and said he "did not much like the idea of the Chinese running up and down the Pacific." Positions were reversed in regard to France. Roosevelt said France should be disarmed and Eden said she should be restored as a European power. Germany, they both agreed, "must be divided into several states, one of which must, over all circumstances, be Prussia." [3]

The conversations were rambling and inconclusive, but of great importance as a revelation of Roosevelt's attitudes. Many of his passing remarks to Eden were soon to broaden into basic themes of policy for the remainder of the war. Later decisions would be based on his easy faith in the possibilities of cooperation with Russia, his annoyance with the claims of small countries and especially Poland, his preference for a postwar world ruled by great powers, his exalting of China's potential and his antipathy to France, and his belief in the need to create a power vacuum in the heart of Europe in the place of Germany.

Roosevelt, who avoided bringing discordant topics into a conversation, did not mention to Eden one of the most significant aspects of his thinking: the idea, encouraged by several of his advisers, that Britain, rather than Russia, might be the principal disruptive force of the postwar world. The President had two vague anti-British apprehensions. First, he feared that the British might return to an old-fashioned scramble for political spheres of influence in Europe, thus frighten the Russians who were naturally sensitive about their security, and ultimately provoke a third world war. Roosevelt also believed that British imperialism, especially in India, would produce explosive unrest unless the colonial peoples were granted independence or placed under trusteeship in preparation for independence.

Notwithstanding Eden's insistence on the importance of cultivating Russian friendship, Roosevelt had many reasons for believing that a serious Anglo-Soviet rivalry for power in postwar Europe was a possibility. There was British procrastination over establishing the second front and reluctance to make sacrifices to maintain the flow of convoys to north Russia. There was also Churchill's obsession with Mediterranean operations that would contribute little to the quick defeat of Germany and his eagerness

---

[3] The account of the Eden mission and the quotations are derived from the record of the conversations of March 15–19, 1943, in U. S. Department of State, *Foreign Relations of the United States, 1943*, Vol. 3 (Washington: U. S. Government Printing Office 1963), pp. 9–41.

to restore the military power of France for questionable political reasons. Above all there was British history: the decades of anti-Bolshevism and the centuries of reliance on the bankrupt balance of power. Roosevelt believed that he could prevent this dangerous rivalry by convincing Stalin that the United States was an unselfish mediator interested only in preserving peace, and not an accomplice of Great Britain ready to "gang up" against Russia. Accordingly, the President suggested to Stalin that they meet alone for confidential talks free from the embarrassment of Churchill's presence.

In order to emphasize the urgency of such a meeting, Roosevelt sent Joseph E. Davies, a former ambassador to Russia (1937–1938), on a special mission to Moscow in May 1943. Davies was an uncritical admirer of Stalin and a man who refused to allow contrary evidence to weaken his faith in Soviet good intentions. Davies flattered Stalin, told American press correspondents in Moscow that any criticism of Russia bordered on treason because it played into Hitler's hands, and showed a Hollywood movie based on his previous experience as ambassador. But he failed to arrange the meeting for the President. Stalin said the necessity of directing the battle against Germany prevented him from leaving Russia. Meanwhile, Churchill learned of Roosevelt's attempt to arrange a meeting from which he would be excluded. The Prime Minister sent a forceful protest to the White House:

I do not underrate the use that enemy propaganda would make of a meeting between the heads of Soviet Russia and the United States at this juncture with the British Commonwealth and Empire excluded. It would be serious and vexatious, and many would be bewildered and alarmed thereby.

Roosevelt, who was sometimes careless with the truth, replied, "I did not suggest to UJ [Uncle Joe, i.e. Stalin] that we meet alone."[4] Churchill let the matter drop, for the President now joined him in trying to arrange a three-way meeting with Stalin.

---

[4] Churchill's telegram of June 25, 1943 and Roosevelt's reply of June 28, U. S. Department of State, *Foreign Relations of the United States, The Conferences at Cairo and Tehran, 1943* (Washington: U. S. Government Printing Office, 1961), pp. 10–11. Hereafter cited as *Foreign Relations, Tehran.*

Not until several acrimonious months of Soviet-Western relations had passed, did this effort meet with any more success than had Roosevelt's separate invitation.

Although denied his meeting *à deux* with Stalin, Roosevelt continued until his death to seek a special personal relationship with the Soviet dictator and to court Russian approval by seeming to belittle his interest in Anglo-American ties. "The President's plan," an American diplomat who worked closely with Roosevelt has written, "was to make the Russians feel that the Americans trusted them implicitly and valued Soviet-American cooperation in war and peace above any other prospective alliance." [5] Prime Minister Churchill described the same attitude as "a strong current of opinion in American Government circles, which seemed to wish to win Russian confidence even at the expense of coordinating the Anglo-American war effort." [6]

Throughout most of 1943 Roosevelt's optimism about what he could accomplish by talking personally with Stalin ran counter to the evidence of Soviet behavior. For example, the Russians were surly and uncooperative recipients of lend-lease aid. They harassed American lend-lease administrators in Russia with petty indignities and refused to provide the basic information on their resources which the United States considered essential if aid was to reach maximum effectiveness. In March Admiral William H. Standley, the American ambassador in Moscow, cabled to Washington:

I am becoming convinced that we can only deal with [the Russians] on a bargaining basis for our continuing to accede freely to their requests while agreeing to pay an additional price for every small request

[5] Robert Murphy, *Diplomat Among Warriors* (Garden City, N. Y.: Doubleday, 1964), p. 210. Quotation used with permission of Doubleday and Company.

[6] Winston S. Churchill, *Closing the Ring* (Boston: Houghton Mifflin, 1951), p. 311.

we make seems to arouse suspicion of our motives in the Oriental Russian mind rather than to build confidence.[7]

The ambassador was told firmly from Washington that there must be no toughening of our attitude. Shortly thereafter Admiral Standley wrote to Roosevelt that perhaps an experienced diplomat should replace him. The President agreed and Standley was recalled.

Soviet recrimination over the delay in the opening of the second front was a more fundamental symptom of bad feeling. Stalin, unmoved by the announcement of the doctrine of unconditional surrender, began the year by complaining of the inadequacy of the military decisions reached at Casablanca. The second front must be launched in the spring or early summer of 1943, he said. When Joseph Davies was in Moscow in May he warned Roosevelt that a failure "to 'deliver' on the western front in Europe this summer" might have a serious impact on Russia's war effort and "participation in the reconstruction of peace."[8] Then Stalin learned of the TRIDENT decisions that the cross-Channel operation would not be undertaken until the spring of 1944. His response to this news was virtually a charge of "deliberate bad faith" by Britain and the United States.[9]

Soviet suspicions were aggravated by the manner in which the United States and Great Britain conducted the negotiations for Italian surrender. The Russians resented that they were not consulted in detail and they expressed uneasiness over the lenient treatment accorded to the reactionary regime of Marshal Badoglio. Did that mean, asked the famous Soviet writer Ilya Ehrenburg, that Britain and the United States would someday deal with Hermann Goering in Germany? The question was unfair because Italy was in no way comparable to Germany in Anglo-American thinking.

Mussolini, in power since 1922, did not excite the same loathing as did Hitler. He was viewed as a comic windbag who had performed useful services for his country until, in the 1930's, he be-

---

[7] *Foreign Relations, 1943*, Vol. 3, p. 510.

[8] *Ibid.*, p. 658.

[9] Robert E. Sherwood, *Roosevelt and Hopkins: An Intimate History* (New York: Harper, 1948), p. 734.

came intoxicated by an antique and unfortunately grandiose vision of Italian imperialism while, at about the same time, coming under the sinister influence of Hitler. The Italian people were regarded with pity and condescending affection. They had been tragically misled by Mussolini into committing a series of cowardly deeds; nevertheless they remained fun loving and humane, quite different from the cold and deadly Germans. Although unconditional surrender theoretically applied to Italy, both the American and British governments implied that Italy would be forgiven if she abandoned Germany. For example, as the invasion of Sicily began in July 1943, Italian cities were showered with leaflets in which Roosevelt and Churchill held out the hope that Italy might regain "a respected place in the family of European nations. . . . The time has come for you to decide whether Italians shall die for Mussolini and Hitler — or live for Italy, and for civilisation."[10]

The response from Rome came quickly. Mussolini was removed from office July 25 and his successor, Badoglio, soon sent out peace feelers through agents in Lisbon, Tangier, and then Madrid. Roosevelt and Churchill now found themselves subjected to the same type of criticism at home and from Moscow which had greeted the deal with Darlan during the previous year. Badoglio was an old Fascist and before falling out with Mussolini in 1940 had led Italian troops in the despicable attack on Ethiopia in 1935; furthermore, he was supporting and supported by an unattractive and antidemocratic monarch, King Victor Emmanuel III. To deal with Badoglio and the King, said outraged liberals, was to give aid and comfort to the very elements for whose destruction the war was supposedly being fought. Military expediency, however, was a stronger argument than doctrinaire idealism; serious armistice negotiations began on the assumption that the Badoglio regime could continue in power.

Badoglio, however, tried to maneuver Britain and the United States into accepting Italy as an ally against Germany rather than the victim of surrender. This was too much. Badoglio was required to accept armistice terms giving the Allies an unfettered

---

[10] Churchill, *Closing the Ring*, p. 46.

right to decide Italy's fate. What they decided was to depend on Italy's behavior and especially on the vigor and sincerity of her resistance to Germany. The surrender was formally proclaimed September 8, 1943. Italy declared war on Germany and was recognized as a cobelligerent on October 13. Italy had succeeded in becoming a semi-ally and thereafter was treated with increasing leniency. She had acted in expectation of finding surcease from the horror of war, but ironically her worse days were yet to come as the German enemy fought a grim two-year holding action along the entire length of the peninsula. Liberation was achieved at frightful cost, but only with the final defeat of Germany.

The Russians were excluded from all participation in the arrangements for Italian surrender and afterwards from an effective share in the management of Italian affairs. Was this a mistake? Stalin said it was intolerable for Russia to be a mere observer while the United States and Britain made agreements for Europe. Some American diplomats warned that later Russia could turn the Italian precedent into an argument for excluding the United States and Britain from a voice in the affairs of the countries liberated by the Red Army. If Russia had been made a managing partner in Italy, would the Kremlin have abandoned its suspicions and later given the West a share in, for example, the political reconstruction of Poland? In retrospect it seems more likely that the Soviets would have exploited their Italian foothold while excluding the British and Americans from eastern Europe with undiminished truculence. Thus, the procedure in Italy probably was prudent, although at the time it was adopted on the basis of immediate military convenience rather than long-range political assumptions. Some postwar observers have gone so far as to condemn the decision to give Russia a seat on the Allied Advisory Council in Italy, a body without executive power. The Russian presence in Italy, it is claimed, gave an aura of respectability to Communism and facilitated the return of the Communist party to Italian politics.

Because Russia was a powerless observer in Italy, occupation policy was a compromise of British and American views. The British, and Churchill in particular, believed that the Italian monarchy ought to be retained as an element of stability.

Churchill also argued that there were few experienced liberal politicians in Italy after twenty-two years of Fascism; therefore, it was necessary to work with and support right-wing figures such as Badoglio. He feared the alternative was Communism. The Americans took a more idealistic stance, urged the establishment of a republic, and were unhappy at working with men like Badoglio. Roosevelt and Hopkins believed that Churchill had a dangerous predilection for monarchies and that his motives in trying to protect King Victor Emmanuel were unworthy of a democratic statesman. After months of Anglo-American fencing over Italian politics, Badoglio stepped down and was followed by a succession of unstable governments of generally liberal hue. Finally in June 1946 general elections and a referendum were held. The Christian Democrats won the largest number of votes and the monarchy was voted down by a 6 to 5 margin in favor of a republic. Thus, American pressure in the long run prevailed.

The contretemps over Italy boded ill for the future. Even more ominous—had Roosevelt been inclined to worry—was the hostility between Russia and the Polish government-in-exile in London. In 1919 the proud Poles regained their national independence and proceeded to attack Russia, then weak from the ordeal of revolution and civil war. The resulting Treaty of Riga (1921) pushed Poland's frontier more than one hundred miles to the east at Russia's expense. The population of the annexed area was varied, but more than half were Ukrainians and Russians. The 1921 line lasted until 1939 when Poland was attacked and partitioned by Germany and Russia acting in collusion. The Polish exile government which eventually established itself in London looked on Stalin and Hitler as equal enemies. Then came Hitler's invasion of Russia and the formation of the Anglo-American-Soviet coalition against Germany. The London Poles opened diplomatic relations with Moscow and tried to forget past hatred.

But the location of the common frontier remained unresolved. The Poles said they could not consent during the war to any retreat from the 1921 line. The Soviets said they insisted upon the western frontier of 1941 as it existed before the German attack. This happened to correspond closely to a boundary suggested in 1919 at the Paris Peace Conference and named the Curzon line after the British foreign secretary who officially sponsored it. A third of a nation lay between. The Poles, with their country under German occupation, had little material power and they lived in constant fear that Roosevelt and Churchill would make a territorial deal with Russia at their expense. Roosevelt had little sympathy for Poland but he was careful to avoid an open concession to Russia, largely because he feared the political power of several million Polish-Americans. His tactic was procrastination and postponement.

Polish Prime Minister Sikorski was tireless in his efforts to change the American position. If Stalin's pretensions are not firmly challenged now, he said in January 1943, Stalin

will take it for granted that neither the United States nor Great Britain are going to lift a finger to prevent the domination at the close of the war of most of eastern and southern Europe by the Soviet Union, and the imperialistic ambitions of the Soviet Union will be greatly accelerated and enhanced.

Roosevelt told the Polish government "to keep its shirt on." [11] The American argument was that Poland's and the world's security would depend on Russia's willingness to cooperate in the postwar world, therefore, the present was no time to make trouble.

Meanwhile, the Russians had arrested the Polish relief agents who were trying to ease the suffering of Polish refugees in Russia. The Russians also were treating as Soviet citizens all those who had resided in the disputed area before the war. In April 1943 a major crisis erupted when the Germans announced to the world the discovery of mass graves in the Katyn forest containing the bodies of 8000 Polish officers allegedly murdered in 1940 by the Russians who held them prisoners. The charge was crude German propaganda, but the Poles suspected correctly that it was true. Katyn appeared to be the grim solution to the mystery of the whereabouts of thousands of officers who had vanished without trace from Russian prison camps. The London Poles spurned advice to keep silent in the interests of Allied unity and publicly requested an investigation by the International Red Cross. The Soviet government said it was being outrageously

---

[11] *Foreign Relations, 1943,* Vol. 3, pp. 317, 329.

slandered, abruptly broke diplomatic relations with the Polish government-in-exile, and soon began to organize a largely Communist clique of Poles in Russia to assume the future government of Poland. After the Katyn crisis, the issue of Polish frontiers became less important than the question of who would rule in postwar Poland: a Soviet satellite regime or freely elected successors to the London exile government.

Some American diplomats were deeply concerned by the many signs of fundamental Soviet suspicion and hostility to the West, but Roosevelt's optimism was apparently unaffected by events. When Stalin refused to meet the President alone or with Churchill, Roosevelt settled happily for the Anglo-American conference (QUADRANT) in Quebec in August 1943. The coordination of military strategy for western Europe was the principal business of this conference, but Stalin's ominous conduct could not be ignored. Churchill saw "bloody consequences in the future." [12] Roosevelt, however, laughed at the Prime Minister's gloom and retained an undaunted faith in ultimate Soviet good intentions.

As if to prove Roosevelt correct, Stalin began to soften his tone and suggested a meeting in the immediate future of responsible representatives of the three countries pending the time when the Big Three conference could be arranged. A few weeks later Stalin for the first time indicated a genuine readiness to meet Roosevelt and Churchill, in late November, provided the meeting was held near the Soviet border in Teheran, capital of Iran. Roosevelt and Churchill agreed on the preliminary meeting on the foreign office level to be held in Moscow, but the President said that the constitutional necessity of keeping in touch with Congress prevented him from going as far as Iran for the major meeting. The outlook, nevertheless, was encouraging. Meanwhile, Secretary of State Hull prepared to go to

---

[12] Herbert Feis, *Churchill, Roosevelt, Stalin: The War They Waged and the Peace They Sought* (Princeton, N. J.: Princeton University Press, 1957), p. 172.

Moscow. Here was his first and only major assignment during the war. The prospect filled him with a sense of almost mystical exaltation. He believed the Moscow meeting would be a turning point in world history.

The Secretary's high expectations grew out of his passionate involvement in preparations for the establishment of a postwar international security organization. Isolated from the President and lacking knowledge of important wartime negotiations, the Secretary found solace in the hope that a new league of nations, fulfilling the vision of Woodrow Wilson, would emerge from the war. Hull believed that the tragic rejection of the League in 1919–1920 resulted partly from Wilson's failure to educate the American people and partly from an evil mixture of partisan politics with foreign policy. His mission was to prevent the Wilsonian tragedy from happening again. With his eyes more on the past than on the harshness of the present, he organized an extensive planning operation centered in the State Department but including important representatives of many segments of American life and leaders of both parties in Congress. By the autumn of 1943 the results of Hull's labors were evident in the overwhelming majorities which passed the Fulbright resolution in the House and the Connally resolution in the Senate calling on the United States to help establish and maintain an "international authority with power to prevent aggression and to preserve the peace of the world." No longer, Hull believed, would foreign nations have cause to question the dependability of the United States. Isolation was dead, and now if the Soviet Union would adhere to a declaration on collective security which he would sponsor at the Moscow conference, the millenium might well be at hand.

The three major powers approached the Moscow conference in different ways. The Russians proposed that the question of an Anglo-American second front be the only item on the agenda. They made it clear that unless they were satisfied on that issue, they would discuss nothing else. The British put forward a lengthy agenda calling for detailed examination of a host of tangled European political problems. Hull opposed the British approach and argued that if the great powers could agree broadly on the idea of collective security, all detailed questions could be easily solved later. He concentrated all his efforts on securing passage of a declaration proclaiming that the powers "recognize the necessity of establishing at the earliest practicable date a general international organization, based on the principle of the sovereign equality of all peace-loving states, and open to membership by all such states, large and small, for the maintenance of international peace and security." [13]

The procedure at the conference was a compromise. First, the Russians were satisfied thanks to skillful statements by the American and British military delegates that a second front in 1944 was a virtual certainty. Then the British brought up a variety of political questions upon which Hull scrupulously avoided expressing an opinion. No specific decisions of importance were reached, but it was agreed to establish a tripartite body, the European Advisory Commission (EAC), to sit in London and consider problems arising out of the liberation of Europe from Nazi domination. The responsibilities and powers of the EAC, however, were left poorly defined. Eden felt the body should be granted broad responsibility, but Molotov and Hull disagreed. The Russians seemed to fear that they might be outvoted and Hull suspected that the EAC, unless narrowly restricted in its scope, might develop into a regional control body for Europe and thus undermine the general responsibility of the future world organization.

Day after day Hull tried to steer the conference away from details and on to the consideration of the general principles embodied in his declaration on collective security, but he encountered a worrisome obstacle in Russia's unwillingness to accept China as a signatory. The American believed it was essential to recognize China as one of the four great powers upon which the success of the world organization would depend. "China is too important a factor," Roosevelt and his advisers agreed before Hull's departure for Moscow, "both now and in the future, both because of herself and because of her influence over British India, to be alienated." [14] The Russians, like the British, were dubious concerning China's power and furthermore

---

[13] *Foreign Relations, 1943*, Vol. 1 (1963), p. 756.

[14] *Ibid.*, pp. 541–542.

wished to avoid jeopardizing Soviet neutrality in the war against Japan before Germany was defeated. But Hull on this one issue was outspoken. He told Molotov that there would be no declaration at all if China was not an original signatory. The Russians relented. On October 30 the famed Four Power Declaration was signed with the Chinese ambassador in Moscow acting on his country's behalf. After the conference adjourned, Hull's jubilation was boundless as he listened to Stalin say privately that Russia would go to war against Japan after Germany was beaten. Unity for global victory and permanent peace seemed complete. Back in Washington in November, the Secretary told a joint session of Congress what the Moscow conference signified: "there will no longer be need for spheres of influence, for alliances, for balance of power, or any other of the special arrangements through which, in the unhappy past, the nations strove to safeguard their security or to promote their interests."[15] The applause was deafening. All that remained to bring the optimism of 1943 to a climax was the much desired but elusive Big Three meeting.

In Moscow Hull had failed to persuade Stalin to make a meeting with Roosevelt possible by traveling farther than Teheran. The President then decided that, contrary to his original belief, he could maintain adequate communication with Congress even at Teheran. He gave in to Stalin. On November 11 Roosevelt left Washington and, after stopping in Cairo for a conference with Generalissimo and Madame Chiang Kai-shek, arrived at the American legation in Teheran on November 27. That evening Stalin invited the President to stay in the larger and better protected Russian embassy. Roosevelt accepted with pleasure and on the twenty-eighth established himself in Russian quarters where he met Stalin for the first time.

---

[15] Cordell Hull, *The Memoirs of Cordell Hull*, Vol. 2 (New York: Macmillan, 1948), pp. 1314–1315.

In four crowded and exhilarating days the President conferred in formal session and informally at meals with Stalin and Churchill and on several occasions with Stalin alone. Secure in the knowledge that they represented, as Churchill observed, the greatest concentration of power the world had ever seen, the three leaders planned amicably for the final defeat of the Axis. Churchill showed his usual interest in a variety of Mediterranean and Balkan operations, but Stalin and Roosevelt together allowed no dilution of the OVERLORD plan. The Russians, for their part, promised to time their great spring offensives in order to give maximum aid to cross-Channel invasion; Stalin also reaffirmed Russia's intention to enter the war against Japan. Military plans, however, were far less important than the political discussions of the conference, for it was in the political realm that Roosevelt, without making a single formal commitment, laid down the guide lines which governed the settlement of the war. Political decisions were technically postponed at Teheran, but the manner of postponement was tantamount to uncritical acquiescence in Russia's aims. The Yalta conference of February 1945 is usually considered the great decision-making conclave of the war, but Yalta merely filled in the outline already sketched at Teheran.

The elements of Roosevelt's position emerged from days of disconnected conversation in which he cast himself in the role of the genial mediator who could laugh at Churchill's prejudices and win his way to Stalin's heart. When alone with the Soviet leader, however, Roosevelt was less than mediator, for he laid great emphasis on American disagreement with Britain. For example, he invited Stalin's support in a general liquidation of British and French colonialism; India, they agreed, was an especially difficult problem. The general impression left by Roosevelt in his private talks with Stalin was that the United States was as likely to side with Russia as with Britain in the event of some future disagreement.

The attitude that Roosevelt displayed toward France at Teheran illustrates this point. In the year since the North African landings, General de Gaulle had demonstrated his ability to win the support of the French people in North Africa, the overseas colonies, and the underground within France. In June 1943 de

Gaulle and General Henri Giraud, the politically inept American favorite for the leadership of French military forces, reached an accord: each would serve as a joint president of a newly formed French Committee of National Liberation with headquarters in Algiers. Giraud's authority, however, was a fiction. In October de Gaulle became sole president of the Committee. Shortly thereafter Giraud, shorn of his nominal military command, disappeared from the political scene. De Gaulle remained without rivals. President Roosevelt reacted negatively to the consolidation of de Gaulle's authority and rejected every suggestion that the United States ought to work more closely with the French Committee of National Liberation. On the contrary, the President supported a tentative plan to govern France after liberation by an official responsible directly to the Supreme Allied Commander whose job it would be "to hold the scales even between all French political groups sympathetic to the Allied cause." [16] De Gaulle naturally expected that his Committee would be directly responsible for the civil administration of France.

The President seemed bent not only on blocking de Gaulle's drive for authority, but on punishing France as a whole for its failure to resist Germany in 1940. On the way to Teheran he told the Joint Chiefs of Staff that "it was his opinion that France would certainly not again become a first class power for at least 25 years." [17] The contrary British expectation, he said, was wrong and merely reflected the British desire to have French military strength at their disposal in the future. Roosevelt developed these ideas in conversation with Stalin at Teheran and stressed most emphatically his disagreement with Churchill. The President commented that no Frenchman over the age of forty should be allowed to hold office in postwar France, thus disqualifying all those in positions of responsibilities at the time of the German victory. He agreed with Stalin that "the French must pay for their criminal collaboration with Germany" and that "the

---

[16] Quoted by Julius W. Pratt, *Cordell Hull* (New York: Square, 1964), Vol. 2, p. 586. This work is the most recent addition to the series on *The American Secretaries of State and Their Diplomacy*, edited by Samuel Flagg Bemis and Robert H. Ferrell.

[17] *Foreign Relations, Tehran*, p. 195.

entire French ruling class was rotten to the core." [18] No decisions were made in regard to France at Teheran, but from the drift of Roosevelt's remarks it appeared that he and Stalin were firmly united against Churchill in their determination to treat France almost as an enemy country and to prevent the reestablishment of military power in France in the foreseeable future.

The future of Germany was the most important topic discussed at the conference. Churchill recommended a moderate reorganization of Germany in order to create political and economic stability. He said Prussia, which he considered the source of German militarism, should be detached and south Germany ought to be associated with the small Danubian states in a confederation. Stalin attacked the idea of a confederation and demanded drastic dismemberment. Roosevelt sided with Stalin and put forward a plan for the permanent destruction of the German state by partition into five weak self-governing parts and the imposition of an international trusteeship over the heavily industrial Ruhr and Saar regions, the city of Hamburg, and the Kiel canal. The preservation of this regime would depend on Russian power, for the President assumed that the American people would demand the withdrawal of American troops shortly after victory. Churchill argued against such schemes, only to be accused by Stalin of harboring a secret affection for Germany. Roosevelt's habit on these tense occasions was to preserve the generally friendly tone of the discussion by giving good-natured support to Stalin. For example, one night at dinner Stalin said that 50,000 to 100,000 German officers ought to be exterminated. Churchill was appalled and stoutly combatted this proposal of "cold blooded execution of soldiers who had fought for their country." Roosevelt, however, tried a macabre joke by saying the figure for execution should be set at 49,000 or more.[19] In the end all agreed that it was too soon to reach final conclusions about Germany and that the European Advisory Commission should be directed to conduct further studies. The rule for Germany, as for every other difficult question at Teheran was: if at first you disagree, postpone.

---

[18] *Ibid.*, pp. 485, 509.
[19]*Ibid.*, p. 554.

All three leaders realized that the future of Poland was a crucial question. Here Churchill took the initiative, saying that Britain had gone to war in 1939 because of Germany's invasion of Poland and was now committed to the reestablishment of a strong, independent country. Stalin, however, blocked effective discussion of Poland's political problems by saying that the Polish government in London was implicated with the Germans and that their agents in Poland were killing partisans. Roosevelt said little on the Polish question in the presence of Churchill, but privately he told Stalin he needed the votes of the six or seven million Americans of Polish extraction in the United States. For this reason, although he sympathized with Stalin's views on Poland, he could not participate in any discussion or decisions until after the elections. Stalin replied that now that the President had explained, he understood.

Many other European issues were also discussed in a tentative fashion short of decision. Roosevelt could truthfully say that he had made no commitments, and yet from the tenor of his remarks it was possible to deduce the future shape of Europe if his implied agreements with Stalin were eventually fulfilled. As one American participant at the conference wrote:

Germany is to be broken up and kept broken up. The states of eastern, southeastern, and central Europe will not be permitted to group themselves into any federations or association. France . . . will not be permitted to maintain any appreciable military establishment. Poland and Italy will remain approximately their present territorial size, but it is doubtful if either will be permitted to maintain any appreciable armed force. The result would be that the Soviet Union would be the only important military and political force on the continent of Europe.[20]

The President did not share these forebodings. He was convinced that Stalin desired to cooperate as one of the four policemen of the world and would maintain that desire as long as the other great powers continued to trust Russia. In that case, no nation need fear Soviet military and political power in Europe.

Far Eastern questions were not discussed at great length at Teheran. Stalin reaffirmed Russia's intention of entering the war

---

[20] Quoted by Feis, *Churchill, Roosevelt, Stalin,* p. 275.

against Japan and indicated that in due time he would expect compensation. Roosevelt agreed that Russia might acquire all of the Kurile Islands and the southern half of Sakhalin from Japan. More important, Dairen in Manchuria could be made a free port in order to give Russia an ice-free outlet and Russia might also regain something of the special privileges enjoyed long ago on the Manchurian railways. Stalin wondered if China would approve of such arrangements, but Roosevelt foresaw no difficulties. Churchill was delighted by this discussion and said "that hungry nations and ambitious nations are dangerous, and he would like to see the leading nations of the world in the position of rich, happy men." [21]

Roosevelt left Teheran on December 2 and, after further conferences in Cairo, returned to Washington in triumph. His personal meeting with Stalin had apparently accomplished all and more than he had expected in his most optimistic moments. The year which opened so auspiciously with the proclamation of the doctrine of unconditional surrender at Casablanca was closing with military victory assured, after which it seemed certain that the great powers would cooperate in bringing stable peace to Europe. Only in Asia did Roosevelt see major uncertainties. Britain and Russia had recognized China as a great power in principle; could they be persuaded to recognize her in fact? Roosevelt believed that China's attainment of her rightful place as the leader of Asia would mean the end of European colonialism. Would Britain and France withdraw peacefully? Roosevelt and his advisers now faced these questions.

---

[21] *Foreign Relations, Tehran*, p. 568.

CHAPTER V

India, China, and Anti-imperialism

HISTORIANS SEEKING to explain the present by the past emphasize those aspects of American diplomacy during the Second World War which show incipient conflict with Russia. They tend to forget that throughout most of the war President Roosevelt and his advisers worried less about the possibility of conflict with Russia than about the continued existence of western, particularly British, imperialism. The President believed that a refusal by the imperial powers to grant independence to colonial peoples was far more likely to produce a third world war than anything that Russia might do. Thus, he embarked on a crusade against imperialism in the Allied camp. This crusade enjoyed a high priority as a task for American diplomacy until the closing months of the war when Russian intentions in Europe were recognized as the greater threat to permanent peace. Also by 1944–1945 Americans were discovering that freedom does not in itself solve the problems of a former colonial people or lessen the world's insecurity.

Anti-imperialism is the oldest ideal of American foreign policy, although the term itself is a product of the late nineteenth century. Since 1776 the United States has deplored the domination of one people by another and has encouraged aspirations for independence everywhere in the world. Although American governments had not always followed the ideal, the Roosevelt administration was staunchly anti-imperialist in word and deed. During the 1930's the nations of Latin America were promised that the United States would never again intervene in their internal affairs and the Philippines was assured of independence in the near future. With the outbreak of the Second World War, the United States applied moral condemnation and material force against the Axis. In the Atlantic Charter of August 1941 Roosevelt and Churchill proclaimed "the right of all people to choose the form of government under which they will live"; and for the remainder of the war colonial peoples used those words as a rallying cry.

After Pearl Harbor, as the Japanese wave of conquest swept over Southeast Asia and threatened India, anti-imperialism became a military necessity as well as an ideal for the United States. "Asia for the Asians," said Japan in an effort to exploit the hatred of dependent peoples for their European masters. At the same time Nazi propaganda was telling the Arab peoples that German victory would bring them genuine independence. In Washington it seemed that the Allies could lose the war if the colonial peoples believed these arguments and cooperated with the Axis. From the American point of view, the Allies had no choice: it was imperative to promise independence for all colonies. Considering imperialism morally wrong, economically wasteful, and a breeding ground for war, Americans also believed that independence would mean a happy, stable, and prosperous postwar world. American tradition, morality, military necessity, and future interest all converged.

The British and French did not share the American concern for the abolition of colonialism. Churchill, for example, announced in Parliament in September 1941 that the Atlantic Charter applied to the enemy, but not to India and Burma; and in November 1942 he made the much publicized remark that he had not become the King's first minister "in order to preside over the liquidation of the British Empire." [1] De Gaulle appeared even more intransigent in his determination to preserve France's prestige and sovereignty over every square mile of her prewar colonial empire. At the highest level Roosevelt and Churchill never allowed differences over treatment of colonial peoples to jeopardize basic Anglo-American unity, but their subordinates operating directly in the colonial areas viewed each other with deep and sometimes irrational suspicion. The typical American representa-

---

[1] Quoted by Ruth B. Russell, *A History of the United Nations Charter: the Role of the United States, 1940–45* (Washington: Brookings Institution, 1958), p. 79.

tive overseas saw the British as arrogant, swaggering snobs determined to maintain their superiority by trampling on the rights of native peoples. The British, in turn, considered the Americans brash, ignorant intruders who preached freedom simply to oust the British and take over the colonial areas for their own selfish purposes. Many Americans during the war favored jovial good fellowship with the colonial leaders, treating them as social and political equals and freely exchanging confidences. The British preferred to remain aloof on the argument that the natives needed to be treated firmly and with discipline. If you abandon your dignity or make unwarranted concessions, the British often argued, you will lose the respect of the people. These differences in national style led to clashes of personnel in the field so bitter that at times the war against the Axis seemed to be forgotten. Fortunately, whenever a crisis arose, calmer heads in London and Washington managed to prevail.

Americans did not agree on how freedom for colonial peoples should be achieved. Some public figures, like Vice President Henry A. Wallace and the 1940 Republican presidential candidate Wendell L. Willkie, implied that immediate independence was desirable and practical. President Roosevelt, however, favored a period of transitional trusteeship on the model of American policy toward the Philippines. "Trusteeship is based on the principle of unselfish service," he wrote in September 1941. "For a time at least there are many minor children among the peoples of the world who need trustees . . . just as there are many adult nations or peoples which must be led back into a spirit of good conduct." [2] Sensitive to the need for delicacy in dealing with the British on the colonial question, he moved by indirection and constantly shifted his ground and opinions. His tactics were the despair of more ardent and doctrinaire anti-imperialists.

Asia, where half the world's population lived under some form of imperialism, was the area of greatest American concern. Since the nineteenth century Americans had looked on their country as beloved guide and protector of China against the selfishness

---

[2] *Ibid.*, p. 43.

of the other great powers. The attitude toward China symbolized by the Open Door notes of 1899–1900 was extended with the coming of the war to include India and the other British, French, and Dutch colonies of Asia. "White nations," said Roosevelt to Soviet Foreign Minister Molotov in 1942, "could not hope to hold these areas as colonies in the long run." [3] The United States also sought to apply its anti-imperial assumptions to the Middle East, but there encountered a cluster of dilemmas. Black Africa was too little known, remote from the fighting, and seemingly backward to attract much attention from Roosevelt or his higher advisers. A few lower-echelon diplomats were aware of the latent turmoil on that continent, but their pleas for the development of an American policy toward Africa were not heard above the clamor of more urgent problems.

Within Asia the initial object of American concern was India, the world's second most populous country and the core of the British Empire. Americans believed Asia would be permanently secure if as a result of the war India was freed and China firmly established as a great power, but American attitudes toward India were contradictory and uninformed. On the one hand, India was a land of romance, of tigers, elephants, maharajahs, and virtuous Kiplingesque Englishmen. On the other hand, an even stronger image was evoked by the saintly Mahatma Gandhi whose only weapons in the fight for freedom were nonviolent resistance and the devotion of his followers. Very little was known in the United States of the bitter feud between the Hindu majority and the large Moslem minority, and less of Britain's complicated efforts since 1917 to prepare India for self-government. Instead of trying to understand the complexity of Indian politics, Americans drew a facile parallel between their own struggle to win independence from Britain two centuries before and current Indian aspirations and capabilities. The parallel had little validity and was bound to mislead.

During the First World War the British government officially declared in favor of the "progressive realisation of responsible government" for India. In the next two decades, however, politi-

---

[3] U. S. Department of State, *Foreign Relations of the United States, 1942*, Vol. 3 (Washington: U. S. Government Printing Office, 1961), p. 581.

cians squabbled endlessly over the meaning of words — what, for example, was "Dominion status" — and blood flowed sporadically in the streets. By 1939 the barrier of misunderstanding between the British and Indian leaders was higher than ever. The outbreak of war, staggering British defeats, and the onrushing wave of Japanese conquest brought on a major crisis. Indian leaders, especially in the dominant Congress party, argued that Britain had dragged India into the war without her consent. India was threatened by Japan, they said, only because it was a British base. Why should Indians die to preserve the British Empire? The British reiterated a promise of Indian self-government after the war, but said that constitutional issues could not be decided while nations were fighting for their existence.

At this stage the American government began to intervene on the grounds that India's fate was vital to the military security of the United States. Secretary of State Hull discreetly hinted in May 1941 to British Ambassador Halifax (who had served as Viceroy of India from 1926 to 1931) that Britain should liberalize her policy toward India, but "nothing came of this approach." [4] In August 1941 John G. Winant, the American ambassador in London, suggested that the United States bring pressure on the British to agree on Dominion status for India, but his suggestion was lost in the argument over whether the Atlantic Charter did or did not apply to India. Americans said it applied universally; Churchill said no. His attitude, which was incorrectly assumed to represent British opinion as a whole, was received with dismay in the United States and angry discontent in India. In October 1941 the United States prepared the ground for further intervention by establishing an American diplomatic mission in New Delhi and receiving an Indian Agency General in Washington. In the sign language of diplomacy these gestures meant that the United States recognized India's potential for independence.

As the military situation in Asia deteriorated rapidly after Pearl Harbor, both Britain and the United States took further steps. Roosevelt tried to discuss India with Churchill in Wash-

---

[4] Cordell Hull, *The Memoirs of Cordell Hull*, Vol. 2 (New York: Macmillan, 1948), p. 1483.

ington in December 1941, but received such a sharp rebuff that ever after he confined his personal comments to the Prime Minister on India to writing. Meanwhile, the Japanese were busy driving the British out of Malaya and Burma. India remained as the only base from which to supply China; early in 1942 American troops established the necessary airfields on Indian soil. With every Japanese victory the desire for passive neutrality deepened in India as did suspicion of British good faith. Churchill considered promising India Dominion status after the war with the right of secession from the British Commonwealth, in other words full independence, but he was advised that the Moslems would consider themselves betrayed by such a development. The Moslem minority feared domination by their Hindu enemies in a unified state and by 1942 were committed to the concept of Pakistan, a separate and independent Moslem realm. The Hindu majority, however, considered the partition of India unacceptable. In the face of these difficulties Churchill withheld a declaration but established a special cabinet committee to study the Indian problem. Meanwhile, Roosevelt maintained the pressure on the British to do something and interjected himself more deeply into the situation by appointing Louis Johnson, formerly assistant secretary of war, as his personal representative to India.

Hoping to break the deadlock and assuage American opinion, the British government in March 1942 sent Sir Stafford Cripps, renowned for his advanced views on freedom for India, on a special mission to New Delhi. Louis Johnson, arriving in India at the same time, hovered at Cripp's elbow and gave the impression that Roosevelt wished to be the mediator between Britain and India. Cripps carried an offer "for the earliest possible realisation of self-government" after the war subject to the right of any province to choose separate independence if it desired and to guarantees for the protection of racial and religious minorities. The British insisted on these conditions in order to fulfill their obligations to the numerous semi-autonomous princely states and their promise that no settlement would be imposed against the wishes of the Moslems. The Congress party rejected the Cripps proposals. Gandhi is said to have called them "a post-dated cheque on a bank that was obviously crashing." [5] The Congress leaders said they would take nothing less than immediate independence without conditions and charged the British with cynically provoking discord between Hindu and Moslem in order to delay independence indefinitely.

Churchill blamed the Congress party for the failure of the Cripps mission, but Roosevelt — who had been informed by Johnson that agreement had been nearly reached — placed the responsibility on the British. In a strongly worded cable to Churchill he suggested that the Indians form an interim independent government along the lines of the American Articles of Confederation of the 1780's. After a short period of trial and error, the Indians could then draw up a constitution for a more perfect union. Churchill, however, felt that such a move would mean "ruin and slaughter." Writing after the war he commented that Roosevelt's "mind was back in the American War of Independence, and he thought of the Indian problem in terms of the thirteen colonies fighting George III at the end of the eighteenth century." [6] Harry Hopkins, in London during this interchange, succeeded in blunting Churchill's annoyance by saying blandly that Roosevelt had no intention of being "drawn into the Indian business except at the personal request of the Prime Minister and then only if he had an assurance both from India and Britain that any plan that he worked out would be acceptable." [7]

By August 1942 the situation, from the American point of view, had reached an intolerable stage. Gandhi and thousands of Congress party leaders had been jailed by the British and attitudes on both sides were hardening. Worst of all were the

---

[5] Reginald Coupland, *The Cripps Mission* (London: Oxford University Press, 1942), p. 52. This brief book by an historian and colonial expert attached to the mission is a clear statement of liberal British attitudes toward the Indian problem as well as a convenient summary of political events in India during 1942.

[6] Winston S. Churchill, *The Hinge of Fate* (Boston: Houghton Mifflin, 1950), p. 219.

[7] Robert E. Sherwood, *Roosevelt and Hopkins: An Intimate History* (New York: Harper, 1948), p. 524.

reports reaching Washington that many Indians were turning against the United States in the belief that the American troops servicing the air lift to China over the "Hump" were in India in order to support British imperialism. Accordingly, a public statement was issued that American forces were in India for the sole purpose of fighting the Axis. Hull then warned Ambassador Halifax that a continued impasse might lead in the United States to "a general movement of agitation against Great Britain and in favor of independence" which would seriously injure Anglo-American relations.[8]

At the end of 1942 Roosevelt decided to send another personal representative to India in order to gather information and indicate American sympathy for Indian aspirations. The man selected was William Phillips, a career diplomat, onetime under secretary of state, and close friend of the President. Phillips spent four months in India and returned convinced that the British were acting in a dangerously misguided fashion. He believed that most members of the cabinet in London, except for Churchill, wished independence for India, but he found the Englishmen in India a reactionary lot blind to the changes taking place in the world around them and determined to maintain British rule indefinitely. Phillips wrote Roosevelt that

there is one fixed idea in the minds of Indians, that Great Britain has no intention of 'quitting India' and that the post-war period will find the country in the same relative position. In the circumstances, they turn to us to give them help because of our historical stand for liberty.[9]

Indian leaders suggested that the United States sponsor and preside over an assembly of all Indian groups to discuss the future. Phillips told Roosevelt that the idea of American chairmanship was a necessary guarantee of independence because "British promises in this regard are no longer believed." [10]

Back in Washington in May 1943 Phillips made an impassioned plea to the President for a forceful American policy.

---

[8] Hull, *Memoirs*, Vol. 2, p. 1490.
[9] William Phillips, *Ventures in Diplomacy* (Portland, Me.: Author, 1952), p. 362. This and subsequent quotations used with the permission of William Phillips.
[10] *Ibid.*, p. 377.

If we do nothing and merely accept the British point of view that conditions in India are none of our business then we must be prepared for serious consequences in the internal situation in India which may develop as a result of despair and misery and anti-white sentiments of hundreds of millions of subject people.[11]

Roosevelt was impressed by what Phillips said, but did not want to risk another Churchillian outburst by mentioning India again directly to the Prime Minister who was also in Washington at that moment. Accordingly, the President sent Phillips to see Churchill at the British embassy and urge that the time was ripe to bring the Hindus and Moslems of India together. According to Phillips, Churchill paced the room in anger and prophesized a blood bath in India if Great Britain made the type of concessions which the United States was urging.[12] Phillips decided it was hopeless to argue. Roosevelt agreed. At that moment he had no desire to place obstacles in the way of Anglo-American agreement on the cross-Channel invasion.

Phillips sought in a variety of ways during the remainder of 1943 to prod the American government into bringing effective pressure on the British. He wrote repeatedly to Roosevelt and he gave impressive testimony before the Senate Foreign Relations Committee to the effect (according to Senator Vandenberg) "that F.D.R. should tell Churchill that he either yields to a reasonable settlement of the Indian independence question . . . or that American troops will be withdrawn from that sector." [13] The President, however, had ceased to appeal directly to the British on India and was about to turn momentarily to Russia for support in his anti- imperial crusade.

At Teheran in November 1943 Roosevelt made colonialism the chief topic of conversation in his first meeting alone with Stalin. The heart of the discussion, as recorded in the minutes, went as follows:

THE PRESIDENT . . . felt it would be better not to discuss the question of India with Mr. Churchill, since the latter had no solution of that

---

[11] *Ibid.*, p. 388.

[12] *Ibid.*, p. 388.

[13] Arthur H. Vandenberg, Jr., (Ed.), *The Private Papers of Senator Vandenberg* (Boston: Houghton Mifflin, 1952), p. 53.

question, and merely proposed to defer the entire question to the end of the war.

MARSHAL STALIN agreed that this was a sore spot with the British.

THE PRESIDENT said at some future date, he would like to talk with Marshal Stalin on the question of India; that he felt that the best solution would be reform from the bottom, somewhat on the Soviet line.

MARSHAL STALIN replied that the India question was a complicated one, with different levels of culture and the absence of relationship in the castes. He added that reform from the bottom would mean revolution.[14]

Having made these careless remarks, based on intuition rather than deep understanding, the President never found another opportunity to discuss India with Stalin. When they met again at Yalta in 1945 too many other topics competed for attention. Meanwhile, the President sought to connect the question of India and all colonialism in Asia with his campaign to make China a great power.

President Roosevelt found a willing ally in Chiang Kai-shek. The Generalissimo was a bitter critic of the British and felt, as did Roosevelt, that the existence of colonialism in Asia played directly into the hands of the Japanese. Chiang also had vague ideas, which Roosevelt encouraged, of playing a role in the departure of the British from India. In February 1942 the Generalissimo and Madame Chiang visited Gandhi in India. Churchill felt compelled to appeal directly to Chiang not to intervene publicly, and Chiang kept official silence. However, he did write sympathetically to Roosevelt of Gandhi's indictment of the British; and later when Gandhi and other leaders were arrested he raised a storm of protest which Churchill deeply resented. "The Government of India," wrote the Prime Minister to Roosevelt, "have no doubt of their ability to maintain order and carry on government with efficiency and secure India's maximum contribution to the war, whatever the Indian Congress may say or do,

[14] *Foreign Relations, Tehran,* p. 486.

provided of course that their authority is not undermined." [15] Roosevelt pretended to mediate, but continued to encourage Chiang to speak out on Indian questions.

Thus, from the start Roosevelt and Chiang were lined up against Churchill. As a result it was impossible for Churchill to distinguish Roosevelt's campaign to establish China as a great power from the Sino-American diplomatic attack on the Asian possessions of the British Empire. The President's repeated suggestions that the British ought to turn over Hong Kong to China strengthened his defensive and resentful attitude. In resisting the idea of China as one of the four great powers, Churchill commented in October 1942 that such spurious status for China would simply mean "a faggot vote on the side of the United States in any attempt to liquidate the British overseas Empire." [16] Americans in turn suspected that the British wanted a weak China in order to protect their imperial position and perhaps even return to the days of European spheres of influence in Asia.

By late 1943 Roosevelt was convinced of the futility of trying to discuss colonialism directly with Churchill, and was placing his hope on China as the main instrument for a solution to problems of Asia. In so doing he hoped to inspire Chiang Kai-shek with a sense of importance in the world, and thereby compensate for the inability of the United States to provide heavy military support for the China theater. There was also a growing feeling in American circles that direct involvement in colonial areas, where we would inevitably be associated with the imperial powers, would tarnish the American image. "By concentrating our Asiatic effort on operations in and from China we keep to the minimum our involvement in colonial imperialism," wrote one of the President's advisers. "We engage in a cause which is popular with Asiatics and the American public. We avoid the mutual mistrust and recrimination over the colonial question, potentially so inimical to harmonious Anglo-American relations." [17]

In line with this advice, Roosevelt wrote to Chiang Kai-shek about his general ideas of trusteeship after the war for colonial

---

[15] Churchill, *The Hinge of Fate*, pp. 507 508.

[16] *Ibid.*, p. 562.

[17] *Foreign Relations, Tehran*, p. 372.

peoples. When it came to specific examples, he spoke more often of French Indochina, then completely under Japanese occupation, than of the British colonies. Roosevelt believed that France was a disgracefully decadent nation which had opened the door to Hitler in Europe and Japan in Southeast Asia. Under no circumstances, he said again and again, should France be allowed to return to Indochina; instead the area should be placed under joint Chinese and American trusteeship in preparation for independence. "France has had the country — thirty million inhabitants for nearly one hundred years," he noted, "and the people are worse off than they were at the beginning." [18] British objections should be disregarded, Roosevelt said, because they were simply afraid of the impact of trusteeship on their own colonies. The President seldom criticized Dutch imperial policy as he did the British and French. This was because of his admiration for Dutch resistance to Germany and Japan, and because the Dutch government-in-exile had promised to convene a constitutional convention after the war to arrange the details of self-government for the Netherlands East Indies and other colonies. The President may also have felt a special kinship with the country of his ancestors.

The climax of Roosevelt's anti-imperialism and of his efforts to flatter Chiang Kai-shek came in November 1943 at Cairo where the two met for the only time during the war. The situation in China was normal, that is, bad and getting worse. Militarily, China was still last on the list of American priorities; the volume of supplies carried by the air lift from India was still a pitiful trickle; and no firm plans had been made to clear the Japanese out of Burma and thus open a truck route into the besieged country. The mutual hostility between the Nationalist government and the Chinese Communists in the north was increasing; only with difficulty had Americans persuaded Chiang not to take direct military action against the Communists. Furthermore, American military experts could not agree on the best remedies for disaster. General Claire Chennault, head of the American air forces in China and favorite of Chiang, urged con-

---

[18] *Ibid.*, p. 872.

centration on bombing operations against the Japanese. General Stilwell, Chiang's gruffly antagonistic chief of staff, argued that air power could do little if the Chinese could not control the ground. Stilwell said the United States should demand that Chiang reform his corrupt and inefficient military machine (for which Chiang hated him) and that a major operation should be launched to liberate Burma (which could not be done because of the demands of the European, Russian, and Pacific theaters together with Churchill's aversion to sending British troops to fight in the jungle).

Roosevelt hoped that these dismal facts could be more than counterbalanced by talking face to face with the Generalissimo. He made a valiant effort, and there in the shadow of the pyramids unfolded the vision of a glorious future for China. Japan was to be driven to unconditional surrender, Korea made independent after a period of trusteeship, and according to the public declaration issued after the meeting: "The territory that Japan has so treacherously stolen from the Chinese, such as Manchuria and Formosa, will of course be returned to the Republic of China. All of the conquered territory taken by voilence and greed by the Japanese will be freed from their clutches." [19] In other words, Japan was to be reduced to the dimensions it had at the time of Commodore Perry. Roosevelt also reaffirmed his determination that China should take her place "on an equal footing in the machinery of the Big Four Group and in all its decisions." [20]

The Generalissimo and the President returned to their respective countries in a heady mood. Chiang soon reported jubilantly to Roosevelt on the effect of the Cairo Declaration in China: "the whole nation is articulate to a degree that has never been known before in unanimously hailing the Cairo Declaration as a sure sign-post leading the Far East toward post-war peace . . ." The President carried the same optimism to the American people in an address on Christmas Eve 1943: "I met in the Generalissimo a man of great vision, great courage, and a remarkably keen understanding of the problems of today and tomorrow . . .

---

[19] *Ibid.*, p. 403.
[20] *Ibid.*, p. 323.

Today we and the Republic of China are closer together than ever before in deep friendship and unity of purpose." [21] But rhetoric cannot long withstand reality. After 1943 even Roosevelt's cheerful faith in China began to waver. As his faith declined so did the vigor of his crusade against imperialism.

Military developments partly explain the waning of American anti-imperial diplomacy. Idealistic sympathy for the freedom of all peoples remained after 1943, but when colonial areas ceased to be threatened directly by the Axis the attention of American leaders turned elsewhere. India, for example, was out of danger in 1944; thus, there was no military reason to antagonize the British by criticizing their inability to reach agreement with Indian leaders. China's military plight remained desperate until 1945, but her strategic importance in the war as a whole declined rapidly during 1944. Originally, American planners believed that air bases in northeast China would have to be established in order to defeat Japan, but in 1944 it became apparent that an advance from island to island across the Pacific provided a quicker and easier route to the Japanese homeland. With this shift in strategic expectations, all possibility of raising the military priority of the China theater was lost.

The frustrations of trying to persuade the Chinese to help themselves, however, did more to change the American outlook than military considerations. Throughout 1943 American observers in China grew more bitterly critical of the Chiang Kai-shek regime. They reported venality and corruption everywhere; stubborn resistance to political, social, and economic reform; low morale; a general unwillingness to fight; and a readiness to sit back and let the United States beat Japan. In many places the Chinese had relaxed into an undeclared armistice with the Japanese and were engaging in trade across enemy lines. At the same time the Chinese Communists in the north were growing in strength. Their land-reform measures were apparently winning the enthusiastic support of the population in the constantly expanding area which they controlled. The morale and fighting ability of the Communist divisions seemed refreshing to Amer-

---

[21] Herbert Feis, *The China Tangle* (Princeton, N. J.: Princeton University Press, 1953), pp. 109–110.

ican observers compared with the sloth and apathy of Chiang's badly led armies. The Communists said they wanted to cooperate with the Nationalist government to expel the Japanese, but month by month Chiang was allocating more of his forces as a barrier against the Communists. Full-scale civil war was becoming an ominous possibility. This would add to the difficulty of defeating Japan and in the long run would shatter the hope of a stable postwar Asia under the leadership of China as one of the Four Policemen.

By 1944 Roosevelt and his advisers recognized that pledges of support for China's future as a great power and intimate exchanges about the folly of British imperialism provided no remedy for China's ills. Huge dollar loans and gestures such as the relinquishment of extraterritorial rights were also futile, for they did not contribute to the political unity of the country. Thus, the United States in 1944 adopted as its first diplomatic objective in China the unification by peaceful means of the Nationalist and Communist forces and for this purpose sent high-ranking envoys to persuade, cajole, and mediate. Vice President Henry A. Wallace, who arrived in Chungking in June 1944, was the first. Few Americans were more outspoken in their dislike for imperialism, and the British variety in particular, but significantly Roosevelt refused the Vice President's request that he be allowed to visit India during his trip.

Wallace, like most Americans who became entangled with China during the war, underestimated the difficulty of bringing the Nationalist and Communist factions together. Assuming that all Chinese shared a basic identity of interests, Wallace told Chiang that "nothing should be final among friends." [22] Chiang said he was willing to grant political amnesty to the Communists if they gave up their separate territory and placed their troops under his command. The Communists, correctly seeing in this proposal their destruction as a separate force, said they believed in the unity of China but insisted on keeping governmental control of their territory and command of their eighteen divisions.

The next special envoy to try his hand at bringing unity to the irreconcilable was General Patrick J. Hurley, one of the Presi-

---

[22] *Ibid.*, p. 147.

dent's favorite troubleshooters and another vitriolic critic of British imperialism. Hurley, who affected the tough manner of an
American frontiersman and lacked a sophisticated understanding
of China and Communism, left for Chungking via Moscow in
August 1944. He soon became convinced that the Chinese Communists were dedicated idealists, similar in many ways to American democrats, and not genuine Communists of the Lenin-Stalin
variety. Hurley, however, was less critical of Chiang Kai-shek
than most American observers, and he assumed in the absence
of clear instructions that it was his first duty to support the
Chiang regime. In seeking to keep Chiang in power and bring
peaceful unification between the Nationalists and Communists,
Hurley was pursuing incompatible objectives. He stayed in China
for more than a year (following Clarence Gauss as ambassador
in December 1944), and was no more successful in advancing
Chinese unity than his predecessors.

As the year 1945 began, President Roosevelt still hoped that
someday China would become a great power in the preservation
of world stability, but on the eve of the Yalta conference he admitted sadly to Churchill "that three generations of education
and training would be required before China could become a
serious factor." [23] Victory in Europe was near, but in China the
military situation was showing only slight improvement. General
Albert C. Wedemeyer had succeeded Stilwell as commander of
American troops and chief of staff to Chiang and by winning
the Generalissimo's confidence (something which Stilwell had
never been able to do) had brought a modicum of efficiency to
a few Nationalist divisions. But reform was too little and too
late. At Yalta Roosevelt decided that China was too weak and
disorganized to be given a direct voice in the settlement of Asian
affairs. Accordingly, he concluded a secret agreement with Stalin
designed to win the war against Japan and to set the pattern of
Sino-Soviet relations in the postwar era.

In later years Americans said many bitter and accusatory
things to each other about events in China during and after the
war. The ultimate triumph of the Chinese Communists over

---

[23] *Foreign Relations, The Conferences at Malta and Yalta, 1945* (1955),
p. 544. Hereafter cited as *Foreign Relations, Yalta.*

Chiang Kai-shek and their emergence as implacable enemies of the United States mocked the ideal for which Americans had fought. Some critics thought that treachery in the State Department and perhaps even the White House was the only possible explanation for what had happened. Their charges, rooted in bewildered ignorance, helped create a climate of suspicion which damaged the careers and reputations of many of the individuals who had helped shape China policy during the war. It would have been fairer to the men concerned and far more accurate if developments in China had been seen as a painful process of education in the complexity of the twentieth century.

The United States approached its relations with China after Pearl Harbor with a set of simple assumptions: the Chinese were willing to subordinate all other considerations to the great goal of victory over Japan; in the future China would prosper if freed from foreign intervention; and all Chinese, if given the opportunity, would choose democracy and unity for their country — in this they were very much like Americans whom they so much admired. It did not take long to discover the inaccuracy of these assumptions, but it proved impossible to find effective alternatives on which to build a policy. The Nationalist government was obviously inefficient, undemocratic according to American standards, unresponsive to suggestions for reform, and unpopular with large numbers of the Chinese people. If China was to become an effective fighting force, extensive changes would have to be made in the character and behavior of the Nationalist government. But what could the United States do if its friendly advice was ignored? Since the war was being fought to prevent nations from intervening in each other's affairs, coercion of the Chiang Kai-shek regime by the United States would be improper and self-defeating. On the other hand, it would be equally improper and distasteful to allow Chiang Kai-shek to use American aid to impose his undemocratic regime (some observers used the word fascist) on an unwilling people. American power by its very existence was intervention whether consciously exercised or not. This fact was not openly faced at the time, for the American government hoped throughout the war that the goals of victory over Japan, nonintervention, democracy, and unity could somehow all be achieved together.

The existence of the Chinese Communists sharpened the horns of the basic dilemma over intervention. Knowing little about Communist ideology, American China experts assumed that the Nationalists and Communists could be brought together, especially if the Chiang regime could adopt more liberal ways. Cooperation once begun would then hopefully broaden into mutual trust and finally into the political unification of the country. Chiang Kai-shek, however, refused to consider any arrangements that would allow the Communists to retain a power base. He disagreed with those Americans who believed that the Communists were democratic, agrarian reformers and not true revolutionaries in the Bolshevik mold. To Chiang they were deadly enemies who would not rest until they had destroyed the Nationalists and secured control of all China. To please the United States the Generalissimo had to give lip service to the idea of cooperation, but inwardly he believed it was essential for him to destroy the Communists before they destroyed him. The United States would take care of Japan no matter what the Nationalist armies did, but victory would be meaningless if the Communists remained.

During the war Americans never fully comprehended the nature of the internal conflict in China, and continued to seek unification by peaceful means. Some diplomats suggested that the United States should end its commitment to Chiang Kai-shek and extend aid to the Communists in the hope that they would create a unified, progressive China friendly to the United States. This extreme policy was rejected. Instead, through the first months of 1945, the United States postponed basic decisions. Victory over Japan was nearer than anyone suspected, but there was no argeement in Washington over how much aid on what conditions, if any, the United States would extend to Chiang Kai-shek after the war. Copybook maxims about the freedom of all peoples from imperialism and China's rightful place as one of the four great powers provided no guidance. Furthermore, as the war against Germany came to an end, the question mark of Russia's behavior in Europe loomed larger in the minds of American policy makers than the imponderables of China.

CHAPTER VI

The Middle East

O PPOSITION TO British and French imperialism was a central theme of American diplomacy throughout most of the war in the Middle East as well as in Asia. If the Middle East fell, the way would be open for the dreaded juncture of German and Japanese forces along the southern rim of Asia, the Axis would gain control of limitless petroleum resources, and the supply route through the Persian Gulf to Russia would be blocked. Americans believed that Allied, especially British, imperialism in the region played directly into the hands of the enemy. They also believed that the United States possessed unique moral prestige with which to counteract the ill repute of the British. "Goodwill toward the United States," observed Secretary of State Hull in 1942, "has become . . . a deep-seated conviction on the part of the peoples in this area, due mainly to a century of American missionary, educational and philanthropic efforts that have never been tarnished by any material motives or interests." [1] The United States, therefore, sought to expand American influence at every opportunity while urging the elimination of imperial controls and the completion of independence for all Middle Eastern countries. It was assumed that leaders and peoples of the region, inspired by the ideals of the Atlantic Charter and looking to the United States for sympathy and guidance, would present a united front against the Axis.

The United States was the last of the great powers to intervene in the political convulsions which in this century have

---

[1] U. S. Department of State, *Foreign Relations of the United States, 1942*, Vol. 4 (Washington: U. S. Government Printing Office, 1963), p. 27.

transformed the predominantly Moslem lands stretching from Egypt to Afghanistan. The American government was relatively uninterested when the First World War spawned or accelerated the developments which have given the Middle East its explosive instability: the final disintegration of the Ottoman Empire, the rise of Arab nationalism, the blossoming of the Zionist dream of a Jewish homeland in Palestine, and the recognition of the region's immense supply of that essential ingredient of modern power: oil. Between the wars American economic and humanitarian interests in the region grew, but politically the United States remained only slightly involved. Meanwhile, the Arab countries, recent appendages of the Ottoman Empire, acquired varying degrees of nominal independence while chafing under British or French control. The Arabs had little sense of common purpose except their hatred of the embryonic Jewish homeland in Palestine administered under British mandate. The Palestine question slumbered in the 1920's but erupted in the 1930's because Nazi persecutions gave new vitality to Zionism.

At the same time, Turkey, reduced to a manageable core, transformed itself from the "sick man of Europe" to the strongest and most nearly independent state in the Middle East. During the war both sides would pay a high price to preserve Turkey's neutrality and friendship. Iran, formerly Persia, also maintained considerable independence between the wars by following the traditional tactic of playing the powers against each other. Germany and Russia controlled no territory in the Middle East but were active competitors for political influence; Germany was particularly successful in the 1930's in establishing a position in Turkey, Iraq, Iran, and Afghanistan, and in appealing to Arab dislike for Great Britain and Jews.

After 1939 the United States began for the first time to take a sustained political interest in the Middle East, but at the time of Pearl Harbor American involvement was still minute compared to the pervasive British influence. Accordingly, the military planners of the two countries logically agreed early in 1942 that the region was a British sphere of responsibility. But no sooner had the agreement been made than Americans began to suggest that the British alter their political behavior to conform more closely to the spirit of the Atlantic Charter. As the American military and economic contribution to the defense of the area mounted, suggestions gave way to veiled demands. The United States is paying the bill, said many American diplomats active in the region, and therefore should call the tune — especially when the British are making enemies with their domineering and insensitive ways.

By 1943 the sphere of responsibility agreement had been replaced by a tacit understanding that American influence, if Washington chose to assert it, was prodominant. The decline of British power, which was so dramatically revealed by the Suez crisis of 1956, was already far advanced. The British, dependent on the United States for their continued existence as a major power, often disagreed with American policies, but in every showdown the British had to give way. As Americans gained responsibility and experience, however, they acquired something of the British point of view and discovered that simple reliance on the precepts of the Atlantic Charter could not, for example, make Russia cooperate in Iran, safeguard strategic oil reserves, or solve the deadly conflict of Arab and Jew.

The first instinct of American diplomats in the Middle East and of their policy-making superiors in Washington was usually to sympathize with those local elements who opposed the British. But time and again this instinct led the United States into painful confusion. It proved necessary to confront a series of different critical situations, all requiring a special response and none amenable to the application of a single theory. As a result American policy in the Middle East became less dogmatic and critical of the British as the war progressed.

Egypt provides a good example of this process. No country had a higher strategic importance for Great Britain. Egypt meant the Suez Canal, the foothold in North Africa, control of the Middle East as a whole, and the route to India. The country, under de facto British military occupation since 1882, was nominally independent and neutral in the war; but in Cairo, headquarters for all British operations in the Middle East, the British ambassador dictated to the Egyptian government literally at gunpoint. Egyptians, seeing that their independence was a mockery, were naturally resentful. A few politicians close to King Farouk believed in Axis victory and were ready to welcome the Germans whose propaganda played on their hatred of the British.

A major crisis came in February 1942 when King Farouk threatened to install an anti-British prime minister. The British ambassador immediately summoned troops to surround the palace and forced the King to accept a British candidate, Nahas Pasha, as prime minister. Americans disagreed on what, if anything, the United States should do. The British were trampling on Egypt's right to conduct its own internal affairs, and yet King Farouk was a dissolute and reactionary monarch surrounded by a clique of politicians who came close to sympathizing with Nazi Germany. Wallace Murray, the head of the Near Eastern division in the State Department and a confirmed critic of British imperialism, believed that the British had blundered and that the United States should formally complain. He argued that Farouk was likely to emerge as "a martyr in the eyes of his people and a rallying point for disaffection, sabotage and attacks directed at the British." Under Secretary of State Welles disagreed. How would we feel, he asked, if the British intervened in our relations with a Latin American country? Murray challenged the validity of the analogy, but Welles prevailed: the United States did nothing.[2] Meanwhile, the crisis in Cairo passed. Prime Minister Nahas cooperated with the British and remained in power until October 1944 by which time the Axis threat had receded.

Iran, long a cockpit of European imperial rivalry, was another strategically vital area in which the United States had to abandon a simple anti-British policy. In August 1941 Russia in the north and Britain in the south had jointly occupied Iran in order to prevent the country from falling under German control. The United States recognized the military necessity of this infringement on Iranian sovereignty and applauded the signature (January 29, 1942) of a treaty by which Britain and Russia pledged themselves to respect Iranian independence and to withdraw

---

[2] *Ibid.*, pp. 68–71 for the Murray-Welles argument which occurred between February 5 and 9, 1942.

their troops six months after the end of the war. The Iranian government, however, distrusted both Britain and Russia and asked the United States for support. The American minister in Teheran and State Department officials in Washington listened with sympathetic and anti-British ears. The British, reported the minister, were seeking a strangle hold on the Iranian economy out of selfish commercial and political motives. In Washington Wallace Murray read these reports and predicted that "sooner or later the United States would have to assume a dominant role in Iran." [3] The American response was to bombard London with unwelcome advice and to fill Iran with a host of special advisers and administrators in order to encourage the Iranians and keep an eye on the British. The United States also extended lend-lease aid directly to Iran, thereby reducing the country's economic dependence on Britain, and took over control of the railroad from the Persian Gulf over which supplies flowed to Russia. Because of German success in disrupting the Arctic convoys, this "Persian corridor" was the only effective way of sending material to the Soviet Union during 1942 and 1943.

The British were more moderate in their attitude toward Iran than most Americans were ready to concede. The real threat to Iranian independence was posed by Russia, a fact which complicated the simple American anti-British outlook. Notwithstanding their pledges to respect Iran's sovereignty, the Russians busily encouraged separatist movements in the northern provinces under their occupation, obstructed the carrying out of American technical aid to Iran in their zone, refused to allow Iranian troops to enter their area to deal with tribal distrubances, and intensified famine conditions by diverting Iranian wheat production. In March 1942 the Iranian government asked the United States for a specific declaration of support against Soviet designs. Here was a dilemma. How could Russia be deterred or even warned without adding to Stalin's already ominous distrust of the West? The United States had to remain silent. As acting Secretary of State Welles explained to the Iranian minister, "it would not only be inappropriate, but positively prejudicial, for this Government — out of a clear sky insofar as it was concerned — to make any

---

[3] *Ibid.*, p. 190.

public declarations concerning the independence and integrity of Iran." [4]

In the face of this disquieting Russian behavior, the United States in 1943 became less critical of the British in Iran and the British more responsive to American opinion. But given the President's overriding policy of making every possible concession to Russia and avoiding all irritating issues in the interests of Allied unity, little could be done to make the Soviets act in a more cooperative and considerate manner. Secretary of State Hull and Foreign Secretary Eden in Moscow in October 1943 failed to win Soviet acceptance for a tripartite declaration on Iran, but Stalin at the Teheran conference a few weeks later acquiesced. Roosevelt, Churchill, and Stalin thereupon issued a public declaration of support for Iranian independence and promised some postwar economic aid as compensation for the country's wartime suffering. Russian deeds, however, continued to contradict their words. In 1944 they bullied the Iranian government in an effort to secure exclusive oil concessions in the northern provinces. Thanks to Anglo-American support, Iran was able to withstand the pressure for the moment, only to see it mount to new heights after the end of the war.

Afghanistan and Iraq, Iran's neighbors to east and west, presented fewer diplomatic problems to the United States. Neutral Afghanistan was a remote mountain land little touched by the twentieth century. Wedged between Russia and British India and fearing both, Afghans looked with sympathy upon Germany from whom they had received extensive technical aid. Potentially, Afghanistan was a trouble spot; it lay in the path of a possible German invasion of India and it could cause unrest on the Indian frontier, thus tying down troops needed elsewhere. Conscious that the British were disliked by the Afghans, the United States moved quickly after Pearl Harbor to develop closer relations with the country. A legation was opened in Kabul in 1942 (Afghanistan in turn opened a legation in Washington in 1943), special arrangements were made to facilitate trade between Afghanistan and the United States, and a group of American teachers and irrigation experts were provided for the country.

---

[4] *Ibid.*, p. 275.

The United States also played the big brother protecting Afghanistan from alleged Russian and British diplomatic bullying. Noting that Afghanistan remained tranquil throughout the war, Secretary of State Hull later felt that the United States had won a friend.

Iraq, lying between Iran and Syria, was close to the scene of combat and, like Egypt, an unquestioned British sphere of responsibility. Great Britain controlled Iraq, once called Mesopotamia, as a League of Nations mandate until 1932 and afterward under special treaty arrangements although the country was nominally independent. Iraqi politicians were intensely nationalistic, generally anti-British, and receptive to German propaganda. In the spring of 1941 an extremely dangerous situation developed for the British. A pro-German politician, Rashid Ali, staged a military *coup d'état*. The legitimate Regent (for King Feisal, a child) was forced to flee for his life disguised as a woman and riding out of Baghdad under a rug in the back seat of the American minister's car. The Iraqi army then surrounded the tiny British garrison at the Habbaniya air base while the Germans prepared to send planes from Vichy-controlled Syria and Lebanon. The United States agreed that the British were justified in intervening with all the force at their disposal. Rashid Ali proclaimed his devotion to Iraqi independence, but his actions were directly serving the interests of Nazi Germany. Under the circumstances British imperialism had to be supported. Heavy fighting broke out on May 1, 1941. Fortunately, the Germans — who were concentrating all their efforts on the coming invasion of Russia — sent insufficient aid. By the end of May the outnumbered British forces had triumphed. Rashid Ali escaped to Turkey and the Regent was brought back to Baghdad. In 1942 the United States made Iraq eligible for lend-lease aid and the next year the country declared war on the Axis.

Syria and Lebanon, lying between Iraq and the Mediterranean, were less tranquil. Here it was the behavior of the French which persuaded the United States that a simple anti-imperial policy was an inadequate answer to the complexity of the Middle East. These two small countries had been detached from the old Ottoman Empire after the First World War and placed under French administration as League of Nations mandates destined for eventual independence. After the fall of France in 1940 they continued for a short time under Vichy control until occupied by a joint British and Free French force after heavy fighting in June and July 1941. Like the Iranian occupation and the Iraqi intervention, this action was taken to prevent the countries from falling under German control. General de Gaulle promised independence to Syria and Lebanon, but held the countries under repressive political control while the British remained responsible for military defense. This dual arrangement produced a violent Anglo-French altercation. The British accused the French of intending to withold independence indefinitely and demanded that the Syrian and Lebanese people be allowed to hold elections. De Gaulle, in turn, denounced the British for encroaching on his authority and said he intended to uphold the honor of France in the Levant at all costs.

By September 1942 the American representative in Beirut, who believed that de Gaulle would use force if necessary, reported that Franco-British relations were at the breaking point. Throughout this crisis some American diplomats said the United States should support the British; but others said British championing of independence was a cynical ruse designed to oust the French in order to obtain exclusive control for themselves. The American position was further complicated until the North African invasion of November 1942 by the desire to maintain relations with the Vichy government which still claimed legal rights in Syria and Lebanon. Thus, American recognition of the independence of the countries would antagonize both Vichy and de Gaulle and might aid an alleged nefarious British scheme. On the other hand, a refusal to sympathize with the ideal of independence would be inconsistent with the Atlantic Charter and might tarnish the image of the United States in the eyes of the Syrian and Lebanese people. The only practical course was a pose of impartiality which was followed with apparent success, for in October 1942 the British and French reached a temporary accord. At the same time the United States appointed a "diplomatic agent" to Syria and Lebanon, a gesture designed to give the appearance of diplomatic recognition while still acknowledging de Gaulle's special position.

For several months relative calm prevailed. In the summer of 1943 the long-postponed elections were held and in both Syria and Lebanon strongly nationalist, anti-French cabinets were formed. When the Lebanese government in November attempted to curtail French rights, de Gaulle caused the imprisonment of the Lebanese president and all the cabinet members that could be found. Churchill denounced these "lamentable outrages" and won American support against de Gaulle. "What kind of France is this," he asked in a telegram to Roosevelt, "which, while it-self subjugated by the enemy, seeks to subjugate others?"[5] The French, faced with the possibility of losing Anglo-American military aid in their rearmament program, freed the Lebanese politicians. Roosevelt and his advisers were now convinced that French imperialism in the Levant was a greater threat than British schemes. Accordingly, in 1944 the United States extended formal diplomatic recognition to Syria and Lebanon while significantly withholding an ackowledgment of France's special position. De Gaulle's heavy-handed methods had converted the United States from an impartial mediator into an unequivocal opponent of France's continued presence in the Levant. Ironically, the British were less critical of French policy in 1944 because of a desire to see France restored as a major factor in the balance of power.

The last wartime crisis in Syria and Lebanon took place in the spring of 1945. The French wanted treaties with the two countries recognizing France's sphere of influence. But the Syrian and Lebanese governments refused to negotiate. De Gaulle thereupon sent troop reinforcements to Syria and presented his terms for a treaty as an implied ultimatum. The Syrians would not retreat and heavy fighting broke out between French and Syrian troops in Damascus at the end of May. The British intervened with military force vastly superior to the French, ordered a cease fire, and compelled the French troops to withdraw from the city. President Truman supported the British and thus, as the war ended, the French imperial position in Syria and Lebanon had been irrevocably impaired.

---

[5] *Foreign Relations, Tehran,* p. 189.

In Saudi Arabia, where control of some of the world's richest petroleum resources was at stake, the United States confronted Great Britain without the complicating presence of another great power. Saudi Arabia was the creation of King Ibn Saud, a tribal chieftain who since 1914 had defeated all rivals and extended his authority over the scattered population. Ibn Saud's rise from the beginning had been encouraged by the British to whom he looked for political instruction and support. He turned, however, to Americans for economic aid and in 1933 granted a vast oil concession in the eastern part of the country to the Standard Oil Company of California. By 1939 the Company had discovered enormous quantities of oil and had begun production on a small scale.

With the outbreak of war the British, anxious to preserve the confidence of all Arab peoples, stepped up their political activities in Saudi Arabia and granted Ibn Saud a large cash subsidy to compensate for the revenues lost by the wartime suspension of the pilgrim traffic to Mecca. The United States, in turn, established diplomatic representation in the country for the first time by opening a legation at Jidda in April 1942 and provided the country with a technical mission to advise on irrigation. At this point mutual Anglo-American suspicion began to mount. Representatives of American oil interests charged that British political activity was designed to oust them from the concession. They argued that, since the British were dependent on lend-lease aid, the subsidy to Ibn Saud was, in effect, an application of American money against American interests. This argument was heeded in Washington and in February 1943 Saudi Arabia was declared eligible for direct lend-lease aid. Anglo-American rivalry accelerated throughout 1943. Ibn Saud sent two of his sons on an official visit to Washington. The United States granted a large loan and late in the year dispatched a military advisory mission, an action resented by the British who had not been consulted. Meanwhile, in Jidda the American minister said his British colleague was trying to turn Ibn Saud against the United States. The Foreign Office denied this charge, but ultimately reassigned its representative at the request of the State Department.

The situation caused grave concern in Washington because it was believed that American domestic oil reserves were nearly exhausted. Continued control of expanded foreign reserves was deemed essential to American security. A government-owned Petroleum Reserves Corporation therefore was established to acquire access to oil everywhere in the world. Headed by the rambunctious Secretary of the Interior Harold L. Ickes, the Corporation made grandiose plans which appeared to threaten private ownership of oil production, the State Department's responsibility over foreign policy, and legitimate British interest above all. The British, on their part, feared that the United States wanted to exclude them from all Middle Eastern oil and denied that they had designs on the American concession in Saudi Arabia. Secretary of State Hull and President Roosevelt were still suspicious and accordingly increased American aid to Ibn Saud in order further to lessen his dependence on the British. The United States in the spring of 1944 also demanded Anglo-American talks on the oil problem at the cabinet level. The British tried to avoid holding talks because they feared their dependence on American aid would put them at a grievous disadvantage.

The United States insisted and after considerable wrangling over conditions the talks took place in July and August 1944. By this time, however, the atmosphere of suspicion was beginning to clear. Each side, noting Soviet ambitions in the Middle East and realizing the region contained enough oil for both, discovered the advantages of friendly cooperation over a rivalry which, if unchecked, threatened to excite public opinion in both countries and damage Anglo-American relations. Accordingly, an agreement was signed, August 8, 1944, whereby the United States and Britain pledged themselves to respect each other's concessions and pursue broad policies of nondiscrimination designed to supply oil to "all peaceable countries at fair prices . . . subject to such collective security arrangements as might be established."[6] The agreement, although never approved by the United States Senate, introduced an era of permanently decreased tension.

---

[6] Cordell Hull, *The Memoirs of Cordell Hull*, Vol. 2 (New York: Macmillan, 1948), p. 1525.

By 1945 the initial anti-British bias of American policy had been softened everywhere in the Middle East, but one agonizing problem remained unresolved: the future of Jewish settlement in Palestine. Nothing in wartime diplomacy so burdened British and American leaders with a sense of inescapable tragedy. In sorrow they felt compelled to deny the cries of Hitler's victims in order to meet the larger demands of military stategy as they interpreted it. The issue was further complicated by commitments to the Arabs which the British felt they could not honorably break and by the counterpressure of American public opinion which sympathized overwhelmingly with the aspirations of the Jews. Palestine ranks with Poland as a question in which diplomacy was significantly influenced by domestic politics.

Modern Zionism, the movement to establish a Jewish state in Palestine, was born in the nineteenth century and became a factor in world politics during the First World War. The British government, having encouraged Arab nationalism as a weapon against Turkey, felt the need to satisfy Jews throughout the world and especially in the United States by supporting the idea of a permanent Jewish homeland. The result was the famed Balfour Declaration issued by the Foreign Secretary on November 2, 1917:

His Majesty's Government view with favour the establishment in Palestine of a National Home for the Jewish people, and will use their best endeavours to facilitate the achievement of this object, it being clearly understood that nothing shall be done which may prejudice the civil and religious rights of existing non-Jewish communities in Palestine, or the rights and political status enjoyed by Jews in any other country.

Few documents have created as much acrimony. Zionists and Arabs, ignoring the carefully qualified wording, saw the Declaration as an unequivocal promise or a base betrayal. The United States, in the person of President Woodrow Wilson, gave vague approval to the Declaration but refused to assume any responsibility for its implementation.

After the war the British assumed a League of Nations mandate for Palestine and tried to govern in a manner which would gloss over contradictory wartime gestures to Arab and Jew. Few Jews migrated to Palestine in the 1920's and the issue of Zionism slowly faded. Then came Hitler's persecutions of German Jewry and the recrudescence of anti-Semitism elsewhere in Europe. Zionism and the flow of immigrants revived. Palestinian Arabs resisted by force and during the late 1930's the British had to put down a bloody rebellion. In 1939, with war imminent, the British government reluctantly decided that the good will of the Arabs and the security of the Middle East would have to take priority over sympathy with the Jews. Accordingly, in a White Paper of May 1939 the spirit of the Balfour Declaration was negated. The British said that Jewish immigration to Palestine could not exceed 75,000 in the period to March 31, 1944, after which immigration would be under Arab control; in other words, Jews would be excluded. The White Paper also restricted the right of Jews to buy land in Palestine and promised eventual independence for Palestine under the Arab majority. If the policy of the White Paper prevailed, the Zionist dream was dead.

The White Paper was so obviously an act of desperation that the Arab peoples doubted British sincerity, and continued to be receptive to Nazi propaganda. Jews, on the other hand, were sickened. It seemed that the British government had sacrificed them because it knew that under no circumstances would they give aid to Hitler. The only course for the Jewish community in Palestine was, in the words of David Ben Gurion, to "fight the war as if there were no White Paper, and the White Paper as if there were no war."[7] This meant offering Jewish units for combat under British command. It also meant the encouragement of illegal immigation, the stockpiling of arms for use within the country, and constant, articulate propaganda against the British policy. When news of Hitler's campaign to exterminate the Jews leaked out of Europe in 1942, the British dilemma became almost unbearable in its cruelty. To give in to Zionist demands might cause the entire Arab world to rise against the Allies; Hitler

---

[7] Quoted by George Kirk, *The Middle East in the War* (London: Oxford University Press, 1952), p. 13.

might win the war. To maintain restrictions on immigration into Palestine meant that untold thousands of Jews would die who might otherwise be saved.

The American government found it impossible to adopt a consistent policy on Palestine. Public opinion in the United States was clear and powerfully expressed. No arguments concerning military expediency or Arab opinion could prevail over the horror of extermination. In the words of a statement signed by 63 senators and 182 congressmen, all of whom belonged to the American Palestine Committee:

it shall be the common purpose of civilized mankind to right this cruel wrong insofar as may lie in our power, and, above all, to enable large numbers of the survivors to reconstruct their lives in Palestine where the Jewish people may once more assume a position of dignity and equality among the peoples of the earth.[8]

On the other hand, as the British were quick to point out, every expression of sympathy for the goal of a Jewish Palestine was resented by the Arabs who claimed, with some reason, that the creation of a Jewish state against their will would be a violation of the Atlantic Charter. The Arabs, however, were unable to influence American public opinion.

Officially, the American government took refuge in platitudes about the beauties of trust, cooperation, and peaceful settlement of all disputes while affirming that full responsibility for decisions lay with the British government. Secretary of State Hull tried to please both sides by declaring: "The Jews have long sought a refuge. I believe that we must have an even wider objective; we must have a world in which Jews, like every other race, are free to abide in peace and honor."[9] Privately there was a tendency in Washington to put the primary blame for the Palestine dilemma, as for other Middle Eastern problems, on the British. Wallace Murray in the State Department condemned the British "for having permitted, and even encouraged, the Arabs to establish a vested right in that burning question." He implied that the British were deliberately creating discord in

[8] *Foreign Relations, 1942*, Vol. 4, p. 550.
[9] *Ibid.*, p. 548.

order to maintain their imperial position in the Middle East and believed it was possible to work out a settlement between Arab and Jew if the American government exerted its influence. "Our reputation in the Arab World is solidly established on confidence and good faith in our motives. This is an asset no longer possessed by the British and one which they should therefore be glad to exploit jointly with us."[10]

President Roosevelt, hypersensitive to the political power of five million Jewish Americans, maintained an active interest in Palestine. He had no precise ideas on how a settlement could be reached, but characteristically made a great many suggestions. In 1942 he was attracted to the idea of winning King Ibn Saud's support for a Jewish homeland by offering him generous economic aid and the possibility of becoming "boss of bosses" for the Arab world. American Middle Eastern experts thought this an absurb idea. In 1943 the President turned to one of his favorite panaceas, trusteeship, and suggested that Palestine should be administered jointly by a Jew, a Christian, and a Moslem — thereby becoming a genuine Holy Land for three religions. He also toyed with the idea of a federal union between Palestine and the neighboring Arab states. He optimistically believed that the Arabs would get over their prejudices and ultimately welcome Jewish leadership and technology in developing the economy of the Middle East for the benefit of all.

As the presidential election of 1944 approached, Roosevelt and Hull came under increasing pressure to define the government's position and to compel the British to modify their policy for the benefit of the Zionists. The British did make a small concession by stating that limited immigration could continue after the deadline of March 31, 1944 set by the White Paper of 1939. This did not satisfy American opinion and early in 1944 resolutions were introduced in the House and Senate calling on the United States government to secure free entry of Jews into Palestine with "full opportunity for colonization so that the Jewish people may ultimately reconstitute Palestine as a free and democratic Jewish commonwealth." Fearing that the passage of these resolutions would create such Arab hos-

---

[10] *Ibid.*, pp. 555–556.

tility as to endanger the lives of American troops in the Middle East, the State and War Departments succeeded in having them quashed in committee. But at the same time the President assured Jewish leaders that he disapproved of the British White Paper and would see that "when future decisions are reached full justice will be done to those who seek a Jewish National Home." Also both major parties inserted pro-Zionist planks in their 1944 platforms, and Roosevelt in October gave a promise that, if reelected, he would find the means of establishing a Jewish commonwealth in Palestine. The State Department did its best to explain away these political pledges issued for home consumption by assuring Middle Eastern rulers that no decision on Palestine should be reached without "full consultation with both Arabs and Jews." But the President, as Secretary of State Hull observed, "talked both ways to Zionists and Arabs, besieged as he was by each camp."[11]

After the election the President neglected the Zionists and during the closing months of his life talked to the Arabs. At Yalta the Palestine question was not raised, much to the disappointment of Zionist leaders who were hoping for a Big Three declaration in support of their goal. Then, on his return from Yalta, Roosevelt held a series of surprise meetings on board the cruiser *Quincy* with King Farouk of Egypt, Emperor Haile Selassie of Ethiopia, and Ibn Saud. Churchill, as Harry Hopkins commented, was disturbed by the President's action "because he thought we had some deep laid plot to undermine the British Empire in these areas." Although there was some justification for Churchill's uneasiness, he need not have worried over these meetings. The confrontations with Farouk and Haile Selassie were largely ceremonial and the talk with Ibn Saud dealt exclusively with Arab opposition to Zionism. Roosevelt listened with apparent fascination as the colorful chieftain told of his determination to end Jewish immigration. "I gained the impression," wrote Hopkins, "that the President was overly impressed by what Ibn Saud said."[12] This seems to have been the case, for back in the United States Roosevelt remarked to

---

[11] Hull, *Memoirs*, Vol. 2, pp. 1534–1536.

[12] Robert E. Sherwood, *Roosevelt and Hopkins: An Intimate History* (New York: Harper, 1948), pp. 871–872.

Congress on March 1 that "I learned more about the whole problem, the Moslem problem, the Jewish problem, by talking with Ibn Saud for five minutes than I could have learned in exchange of two or three dozens letters."[13] The remark was typical Roosevelt flippancy, but it sounded ominous to Zionist ears.

One month later Roosevelt was dead. Meanwhile, Germany was going down to defeat and as Allied armies occupied the country the full story of the gas chambers, crematoria, and extermination camps was revealed to the world. President Harry S. Truman, unschooled in the thousands of problems confronting him, reacted in a humane and compassionate way. The surviving remnant should be immediately admitted to Palestine, he said. The British, trying to subdue a wave of Zionist terrorism in Palestine, pleaded for time. In August 1945 Prime Minister Clement Atlee (who had succeeded Churchill after the Labour party's victory in the July 1945 elections) suggested to Truman that an Anglo-American committee of inquiry be sent to Palestine. The President agreed, but thereafter American policy became increasingly Zionist. When the state of Israel after three more years of bloodshed and turmoil declared its independence in 1948, the United States was the first country to extend diplomatic recognition. The Zionist dream was fulfilled, but the conflict between Jew and Arab remained as a primary cause of instability in the Middle East.

Turkey was the only Middle Eastern country fortunate and skillful enough to maintain more than nominal independence during the war; it was also the only country of the region in which the United States and Great Britain did not suspect each other's motives. There was some friendly Anglo-American rivalry for diplomatic prestige and occasional disagreement over methods, but since neither country could impose its will on Turkey, they cooperated quite well through four years of delicate and highly involved diplomacy.

---

[13] Quoted by Kirk, *The Middle East in the War*, p. 327.

The old Ottoman Empire, defeated and discredited during the First World War, disappeared in 1918. Kemal Ataturk, a brilliant political tactician, then led the country through a social, economic, and political revolution. By the time of his death in 1938 he had created in Turkey the rudiments of a modern state. Ataturk's lieutenants, who governed during the war, sought to protect that achievement and to maintain Turkey's independence regardless of which side won the great struggle raging around her borders. With a total disregard for sentimentality, the Turks attained their goal by exploiting the bargaining power of her strategic location as the bridge between Europe and the Middle East, her control of the Dardanelles, her economic resources, and her experienced (although poorly equipped) army. Slippery masters of equivocation, procrastination, and calculated vacillation, they teetered between Axis and Allies and won favors from both before finally declaring war against Germany in February 1945 just in time to receive an invitation to the United Nations conference in San Francisco. These tactics infuriated British and American diplomats while at the same time compelling a grudging admiration.

In the first years of the war, Turkey balanced a nonaggression pact with Germany (1941) against a defensive alliance with Britain (1939), and received lend-lease aid from the United States. Neither side could afford to support her if she entered the war or endure the damage that she could inflict as an enemy. Thus, through 1942 both paid for her neutrality by supplying arms, economic aid, and high prices for Turkish products. Early in 1943 Churchill, enraptured by his perennnial vision of a great campaign in the eastern Mediterranean and Balkans, decided the time had come to bring Turkey into the war. Roosevelt at Casablanca told the Prime Minister to "play the hand"[14] and see what he could do. Accordingly, Churchill went to Turkey in January 1943 for conferences with President Ismet Inonu. Churchill was beguiled into thinking he had accomplished his mission when actually Inonu seems to have used the Churchill talks as a lever to get better treatment from Germany.

---

[14] Winston S. Churchill, *The Hinge of Fate* (Boston: Houghton Mifflin, 1950), p. 699.

British, American, and Russian leaders agreed at the end of 1943 to ask Turkey again to enter the war. The request, culminating in a Roosevelt-Churchill-Inonu meeting in Cairo in December, failed because the Turks were able to exploit small differences in attitude between the United States and Great Britain. Roosevelt, shifting from the position he had taken at Casablanca, now wanted to assert his primacy in diplomacy with Turkey. His instinctive method was to hint that the United States was more sensitive to Turkish needs than Britain. Turkey's position was that she was eager to go to war provided the Allies could protect her from German attack. She then made exorbitant demands for equipment and air cover. American military planners, dubious of Turkey's usefulness as a belligerent and dogmatically opposed to Churchill's eastern strategy, were unwilling to divert resources from the build-up for the cross-Channel invasion. Meanwhile, Germany, informed of every Allied move by a spy in the British embassy in Ankara, applied successful counterpressure.

Thus, as the date approached for the invasion of France, Turkey was still neutral. She was also still receiving aid from both sides and was supplying Germany with chrome, a material vital for the production of armament steel. At last Britain and the United States decided to get tough. Military aid was curtailed and Turkey was threatened with a blockade if she refused to end the chrome shipments to Germany. Turkey complied. The success of the cross-Channel invasion then removed all doubt as to which side would win. In August 1944 Turkey broke diplomatic relations with the Axis and in February 1945 declared war on Germany.

The United States began its wartime diplomacy in the Middle East with the confident theory that opposition to imperialism would help defeat the Axis and ensure lasting peace. By 1945 the Axis threat was gone and British and French imperial power had been radically reduced, but the region was as explosively insecure as it had been on the day of Pearl Harbor. By 1945 it was clear to most American leaders, if not quite yet to the public, that the Middle East—like the world as a whole—was too full of contradictions and uncertainty for diplomacy by slogan. Reality too often forced a choice between evils.

CHAPTER VII

The Future of Germany

UNTIL 1944 MILITARY NECESSITY gave orders to American diplomacy. Busy leaders concentrated on defeating the Axis and avoided thinking deeply about the precise shape of the postwar world. As long as Nazi Germany held the continent of Europe from the Russian plain to the English Channel, President Roosevelt and many of his advisers rested comfortably with their vague and untested assumptions about the utopia that would emerge after Hitler's ruthless day was done. Thanks to the peaceable cooperation of the Four Policemen, they mused, war and selfish national rivalries would be banished. Democracy would become a universal blessing and all nations would cooperate politically and economically for the benefit of mankind.

The climax of this unrealistic optimism came, it will be recalled, late in 1943 when Roosevelt, Churchill, and Stalin met at Teheran. In the glow of military success the Big Three put aside their earlier squabbles over strategy and amiably looked ahead. Prime Minister Churchill felt some uneasiness over how the Soviet Union would behave once the Red Army rolled into central Europe, but the President appeared to have no qualms. The tide of victory had not yet surged far enough to put his happy assumptions about Soviet-Western cooperation in liberated Europe to the test. But with the successful cross-Channel invasion of June 1944 and the simultaneous Soviet advance through Poland, diplomacy entered a new phase. Soon the Allies would be on German soil. Victory was almost in hand. The time had come to give practical substance to vague hopes. What would the victors do with the vanquished enemy and with the surrounding belt of liberated states? As American leaders tried to find answers to that question, their optimistic assumptions came under heavy and often bewildering strain. They did not succeed before war's end in adjusting to the new and disillusioning conditions which confronted them, but, as in Asia and the Middle East, they learned some painful lessons.

Germany was first priority for postwar planners as for military strategists. Everyone agreed that Germany must be permanently deprived of the power to make war, and that all traces of the Nazi system must be eradicated. They could not agree, however, on the proper means to these ends or on the relationship which ought to exist between postwar Germany and the rest of Europe. So profound was the disagreement within the American government that the United States as late as the Yalta conference of February 1945 was still without a consistent, thoroughly reasoned program for Germany. Thus, it became necessary in the hectic, final days of victory to accept a cluster of improvised arrangements with Russia which, as later came to be realized, were not in the best interests of the United States.

President Roosevelt shared the American public's conviction that no treatment was too harsh for the Nazi enemy. Confident that he had an intuitive understanding of Germany, he made little attempt to explore the implications of his determination to split the country into fragments. At Teheran he had casually outlined his personal scheme for drastic partition and had supported Stalin's opposition to Churchill's moderation. Nothing was decided at Teheran, although the newly created European Advisory Commission was assigned the task of working out details for the forthcoming tripartite occupation of Germany. Within a year the EAC had drafted an instrument of surrender, marked out zones of occupation for the three powers, and recommended the establishment of a Control Council to exercise overall supervision while the national commanders retained supreme authority in the separate zones. These were matters of outward form; matters of substance, including the crucial issue of dismemberment, remained undecided. Meanwhile, in Washington three departments—State, War, and Treasury—were competing for the decisive voice in the formulation of American policy toward Germany. Roosevelt remained aloof from the

GERMANY IN DEFEAT

internal debate and by his lack of leadership intensified the conflict among his advisers.

Officers of the State Department felt that the primary responsibility for advising the President on German policy was theirs. By late 1943 the Department had reached the moderate conclusions which it maintained throughout the war. An important memorandum of September 23, 1943, for example, argued that Germany should be granted a tolerable standard of living and an opportunity for economic recovery. Forced partition was folly, for it would create a lasting grievance and thus might lead to new threats of war. The nation should remain unified, but under a decentralized federal government. A healing peace would leave a minimum of bitterness and would contribute to the reconstruction of Europe as a whole. The Army, preparing for occupation duty, reached similar moderate conclusions. The spirit of the Army's draft *Handbook for Military Government in Germany*, completed in the spring of 1944, was sympathetic to reform rather than vengeful punishment. Germany was to retain her centralized administration and much of her industry, which was essential to the well-being of the European economy. After a short period of occupation American troops would withdraw and Germany, de-Nazified and demilitarized, could govern herself. This early planning was calm, humane, and constructive, but it suffered from two fatal flaws: it was out of tune with public opinion inflamed by the war and Nazi atrocities and it did not enjoy the support of the President whose mind, through the first eight months of 1944, was on other things.

The man who compelled the President to turn his attention to German policy was Henry Morgenthau, Jr., the Secretary of the Treasury. Conscious that finance was the fuel of wartime foreign policy, Morgenthau and a corps of energetic assistants had steadily expanded the Treasury's role in foreign affairs at the expense of the State Department, a fact keenly resented by Secretary of State Hull. Morgenthau, friend and neighbor to Roosevelt at Hyde Park, also enjoyed more personal influence with the President than any other member of the cabinet. Thus, when he decided to intervene on the German question, the Secretary of the Treasury's impact was startling and immediate.

During the summer of 1944 while the President postponed consideration of German policy on the theory that nothing need be decided prior to the next Big Three meeting, Morgenthau and his assistants took critical note of the trend of thinking in the State and War Departments. Morgenthau was particularly appalled by the Army's draft *Handbook*. On a flying trip to Europe in August he conferred with General Eisenhower and Ambassador John G. Winant, the American representative on the EAC, and then returned to Washington determined to force a showdown. He showed the offending *Handbook* to Roosevelt and argued that unless the direction of American planning was radically changed Germany would emerge from the war with her power to commit aggression intact. The President agreed. "It is of the utmost importance that every person in Germany should realize that this time Germany is a defeated nation,"

Roosevelt said in a scolding memorandum for Secretary of War Henry L. Stimson. "I do not want them to starve to death, but . . . if they need food to keep body and soul together beyond what they have, they should be fed three times a day with soup from Army soup kitchens . . . they will remember that experience all their lives."[1]

Morgenthau, heartened by the President's support, carried on his fight in a special cabinet committee on Germany consisting of himself, Hull, and Stimson. The detailed Treasury plans, as they unfolded early in September, ran parallel to the extreme suggestions put forward by Roosevelt and Stalin at Teheran. Germany should be required to pay heavy reparations in kind and through forced labor. Large slices of territory should be distributed among Germany's neighbors: the area north of the Kiel Canal to Denmark; the Saar and much of the Rhineland to France; East Prussia and southern Silesia to Russia and Poland. The remaining core should be partitioned into two weak, rural states and an industrial sector under international control which

should not only be stripped of all presently existing industries but so weakened and controlled that it cannot in the foreseeable future become an industrial area — all industrial plants and equipment not destroyed by military action shall either be completely dismantled or removed from the area or completely destroyed, all equipment should be removed from the mines and the mines shall be thoroughly wrecked.[2]

Stimson, Hull, and their assistants considered that the Treasury's ideas were dangerous folly. Such treatment, they argued, would require permanent military occupation of Germany. More important, it would do enormous damage to the economy of Europe wihch could not function without German industry. "This war more than any previous war has caused gigantic destruction," Stimson observed.

---

[1] Cordell Hull, *The Memoirs of Cordell Hull*, Vol. 2 (New York: Macmillan, 1948), p. 1603.

[2] *Ibid.*, p. 1605. After his resignation from the cabinet in 1945, Morgenthau published a clear statement of his "Plan" in *Germany Is Our Problem* (New York: Harper, 1945).

The need for the recuperative benefits of productivity is more evident now than ever before throughout the world. Not to speak of Germany at all or even of her satellites, our allies in Europe will feel the need of the benefit of such productivity if it should be destroyed.

Recovery must come quickly, he added, "to avoid dangerous convulsions in Europe."[3] The Secretary of War was there hinting at a theme which many Americans considered misguided: that stability and a reasonable standard of living were necessary to prevent the Communization of Europe.

Stimson, deeply disturbed by the ascendancy of the Morgenthau program, went to Roosevelt in order to plead for moderation. The interview, on the eve of the President's departure for the second Quebec conference with Churchill, filled the Secretary with despair. His diary tells the story:

I have been much troubled by the President's physical condition. He was distinctly not himself Saturday. He had a cold and seemed tired out. I rather fear for the effects of this hard conference upon him. I am particularly troubled . . . that he is going up there without any real preparation for the solution of the underlying and fundamental problem of how to treat Germany. . . . I hope the British have brought better trained men with them than we are likely to have to meet them.[4]

Roosevelt took no one to Quebec specifically to advise on German policy. Stimson remained in Washington. So did Secretary of State Hull whose nonparticipation was rationalized by the fact of poor health (although it is difficult to say whether he was neglected because ill or ill because neglected). Suddenly, as the conference opened, Roosevelt sent for Morgenthau.

The Secretary of the Treasury flew to Quebec and plunged immediately into separate, but tacitly connected, discussions with Churchill on the treatment of Germany and postwar American aid to Britain. At first the Prime Minister resisted Morgenthau's drastic proposals for Germany. He said he had no intention of seeing Britain chained to a dead body. Morgenthau, however, tried to tempt the Prime Minister with

---

[3] Henry L. Stimson and McGeorge Bundy, *On Active Service in Peace and War* (New York: Harper, 1948), p. 572. This and subsequent quotations from Stimson and Bundy used with the permission of Harper and Row.
[4] *Ibid.*, p. 575.

the vision of British export trade booming thanks to the elimination of Germany competition. It seems doubtful that Churchill
was persuaded by such naive neomercantilism. What did move
him was the accord signed on September 15, 1944 by which
the United States tentatively agreed to supply Britain with $6.5
billion in postwar aid. On the same day Churchill surrendered
to Morgenthau ("from whom we had much to ask")[5] in regard
to Germany. The Prime Minister dictated a short memorandum
incorporating the essence of what soon became known as the
Morgenthau Plan. "This programme for eliminating the war-
making industries in the Ruhr and in the Saar," concludes the
memorandum, "is looking forward to converting Germany into
a country primarily agricultural and pastoral in its character."
Churchill and Roosevelt then initialed their agreement: "O.K.
F.D.R. W.S.C. 15/9."[6] Morgenthau later denied that he and
Churchill had bargained American aid to Britain for British
support for his drastic plan. Technically, there was no bargain,
and yet it is hard to conceive of one agreement having been
reached without the other.

Morgenthau's triumph marked only the first round in the
battle over Germany policy. Back in Washington, Hull and
Stimson prepared the counterattack. At the same time the
Morgenthau plan, whose substance had been leaked to the press,
was receiving far more public criticism than approval, while
in Germany the Nazi propaganda machine found itself with a
highly exploitable issue. The Germany people were told that
the Morgenthau proposal was a "satanic plan of annihilation"
inspired by Jews; Germany had no alternative but to fight to
the death.[7] Roosevelt, sensitive to the need to avoid controversy
on the eve of the presidential election, began to waver. He
wrote to Hull on September 29 that "No one wants to make
Germany a wholly agricultural nation again, and yet somebody
down the line has handed this out to the press. I wish we

---

[5] Winston S. Churchill, *Triumph and Tragedy* (Boston: Houghton Mifflin,
1953), p. 156.

[6] Stimson and Bundy, *On Active Service*, p. 577.

[7] Forrest C. Pogue, *The Supreme Command* (Washington: U. S. Government
Printing Office, 1954), p. 342. This is a volume in the official history of
the *United States Army in World War II*.

could catch and chastise him."[8] To Stimson the President admitted that he had signed the Quebec memorandum without much thought and that he now believed that "Henry Morgenthau pulled a boner."[9] Characteristically, the President decided that the best way out of an embarrassing situation was postponement. "I dislike making detailed plans for a country which we do not yet occupy," he wrote to Hull on October 20.[10]

Thus, as the second Big Three meeting, arranged for Yalta in the Crimea, drew near, American policy was still in flux. Preliminary agreement, however, had been reached on the zones of Germany which the three powers would occupy. Initially, the British proposed that Russia occupy eastern Germany, Britain the northwest, and the United States the southwest. All agreed on the Russian zone, but Roosevelt refused to have American troops in the southwest, a region dependent on lines of communication through France. The President was obsessed with the idea that France after the war would be convulsed by revolution and he feared that American troops in southwest Germany might be trapped. He wanted the American zone in the northwest with direct lines of communication and escape through the North Sea ports. Postwar France was Britain's problem, he said, and the United States was determined to keep hands off. The British were distressed by Roosevelt's arguments. They pointed out that American armies were advancing toward Germany on the southern flank with the British on the north. Chaos would result from any attempt to switch places for the occupation. They also argued that France after the war would be a strong and stable partner, not a victim of revolution. After months of argument a compromise was worked out. The United States took the southwestern zone plus an enclave enclosing the ports of Bremen and Bremerhaven in the northwest. The three powers agreed that Berlin, deep within the Russian zone, was to be divided into sectors and jointly occupied. The question of a Russian guarantee of access rights from the West into

---

[8] U. S. Department of State, Foreign Relations, The Conferences at Malta and Yalta, 1945 (Washington: U. S. Government Printing Office, 1955), p. 155.

[9] Stimson and Bundy, On Active Service, p. 581.

[10] Foreign Relations, Yalta, p. 158.

Berlin was deferred on the theory that arrangements could be made more easily when Germany was actually in Allied hands.

The decision not to press Russia for an agreement on access rights was challenged by some American diplomats, most notably by Robert Murphy who was then serving as political adviser to General Eisenhower. Murphy argued that the Russians were sharp bargainers who would take advantage of the West at every opportunity. Winant, in his capacity as American representative on the EAC, listened to Murphy but vehemently refused to reopen the issue. Acting fully in the spirit of President Roosevelt's unshaken assumption that Russia could and should be trusted, Winant said that Russian suspicions would be aroused if the United States seemed to question their good faith by demanding a written agreement.[11]

The argument between Murphy and Winant was symptomatic of a rapidly developing division of opinion within the American government as a whole. Roosevelt still believed that he could "handle Stalin" and that the Russians would soon abandon their difficult ways and cooperate happily with the West if every possible consideration was given to their requests and if absolutely nothing was done to cause them to be suspicious. The President, and the influential advisers who agreed with him, looked on criticism of Russia as a disservice to the cause of Allied unity and future world peace. They were particularly unreceptive to British complaints about Soviet intententions, regarding them as part of a sinister scheme to inveigle the United States into joining Britain in the old balance of power game against Russia. According to this dominant viewpoint, the United States ought to mediate between Britain and Russia, convincing the one to renounce its inclination to think in terms of building a power bloc against Russia and persuading the other that it could safely cast away its suspicions of the West.

By the end of 1944, however, an increasing number of Americans were beginning to argue that this attitude was dangerously

---

[11] Robert Murphy, in his *Diplomat Among Warriors* (Garden City, N. Y.: Doubleday, 1964), p. 232, writes critically of "Winant's grave responsibility for the personal diplomacy which he exercised in the Advisory Commission negotiations," but it scarcely seems fair to condemn Winant personally for so accurately reflecting the attitudes of President Roosevelt, his chief.

unrealistic. The time has come, said these dissenters, to face the fact that the Russians intend to take whatever they can get and regard American acquiescence as weakness. While giving lip service to such ideals as democracy and national self-determination, the Soviet government would use every means at its disposal to dominate as much of Europe as possible. "It is particularly noteworthy," observed Amabassador Averell Harriman from Moscow, "that no practical distinction seems to be made in this connection between members of the United Nations whose territory is liberated by Soviet troops and ex-enemy countries which have been occupied."[12] Harriman and others argued that it was imperative for the United States to have a realistic understanding of Soviet intentions and to bargain accordingly. It was foolish to give and give, and never ask. "In all cases where our assistance does not contribute to the winning of the war," suggested the head of the American military mission in Moscow, "we should insist on a *quid pro quo*. . . . When our proposals for collaboration are unanswered after a reasonable time, we should act as we think best and inform them of our action."[13] President Roosevelt, however, showed little outward sign of heeding such advice, and as a result filled some Americans with a sense of angry desperation. Secretary of the Navy James Forrestal, for example, wrote in September 1944 to a friend

that whenever any American suggests that we act in accordance with the needs of our own security he is apt to be called a god-damned fascist or imperialist, while if Uncle Joe suggests that he needs the Baltic Provinces, half of Poland, all of Bessarabia and access to the Mediterranean, all hands agree that he is a fine, frank, candid and generally delightful fellow who is very easy to deal with because he is so explicit in what he wants.[14]

This unresolved difference of opinion in regard to Russia had direct bearing on American policy toward Germany. One

---

[12] *Foreign Relations, Yalta*, p. 450.

[13] *Ibid.*, p. 449.

[14] Walter Millis (Ed.), *The Forrestal Diaries* (New York: Viking, 1951), p. 14. This and subsequent quotations from *The Forrestal Diaries* used with the permission of the Viking Press.

attitude suggested that Roosevelt at Yalta should go down the line in supporting Stalin's views on Germany and thereby ensure Soviet trust and cooperation. The other attitude suggested that Roosevelt should move warily, listen carefully to what Churchill had to say, and be prepared to resist excessive Soviet demands. On the one hand he should seek the permanent destruction of Germany as a factor in European politics and confidently allow Russia to acquire a monopoly of military power on the continent. On the other hand he should aim at the preservation of German economic strength as the nucleus of a reconstructed Europe strong enough to resist Soviet expansion in the event that Russian intentions proved hostile to the West. The President, as he prepared to leave for Yalta after the inauguration to the fourth term, had retreated from the extreme position of the Morgenthau plan but he was far from ready to shape policy toward Germany in terms of opposition to Russia.

Prime Minister Churchill was deep in gloom on the eve of Yalta. "This may well be a fateful conference," he wrote to Roosevelt in January 1945, "coming at a moment when the great allies are so divided and the shadow of the war lengthens out before us. At the present time I think the end of this war may well prove to be more disappointing than was the last."[15] Churchill was particularly disturbed by the American refusal to let postwar political considerations influence the shape of the final attack on Germany. He argued, for example, that an Anglo-American force should land at the head of the Adriatic and strike northward into the valley of the Danube in order to prevent as much of western Europe as possible from falling into Russian hands. The United States rejected this plan, and instead ordered the further transfer of troops from the Mediterranean to northwestern Europe. On the main front British military planners advocated a strategic spear thrust by fast compact units across northern Germany to Berlin. This idea, with its strong political overtones in relation to Russia, was also rejected in favor of General Eisenhower's preference for a slow, conservative advance on a broad front—a safe policy which risked no

---

[15] *Foreign Relations, Yalta*, p. 31.

unnecessary lives and assumed that it made no difference whether Russian or Western troops got to Berlin first. Adding to Churchill's woe was Roosevelt's repeated insistence that he would have to withdraw American troops from Europe as fast as transportation could be found to take them home after victory.

Ironically, both Roosevelt and Churchill were letting history determine their opinions while simultaneously urging the other to lead his country in an escape from the past. Roosevelt, fearing a repetition of 1919–1920 when President Wilson had been repudiated by a nation retreating into political isolation, was sure that public opinion would prevent him from committing American troops to postwar duty in Europe. He did not deny that American withdrawal would leave Russia dominant on the continent, especially if Germany were reduced to permanent impotence, but he hoped that Russian benevolence would make her power an asset rather than a threat to American security and world peace. Churchill, wedded to the British tradition of opposing the domination of Europe by any single power, thought that Roosevelt's readiness to trust Russia was unrealistic. If Western values were to survive, the Prime Minister maintained, the United States would have to abandon its historical isolation and take on permanent responsibility for maintaining in partnership with Britain the balance of power in Europe. Roosevelt avoided direct argument with Churchill on this issue, but his most trusted advisers developed the American rebuttal that British reliance on the balance of power had led to centuries of human misery. Now Britain must abandon her historical tradition and put her trust in a world security organization based on full cooperation of the four great powers. As the President and Prime Minister flew in their separate planes over the Black Sea to Yalta on February 3, 1945, neither was ready to accept the other's point of view; each was preparing to argue for that program for postwar Germany which best suited his concept of what the future held in store, particularly the future of Soviet-Western relations. Whether either would modify his views would depend not on their powers of mutual persuasion but on the realities of Russian behavior.

President Roosevelt was a dying man at Yalta. No one realized this at the time, but photographs and the testimony of those who were there bear witness to his haggard, shrunken appearance. His once strong face was flabby and dark with fatigue. His broad shoulders drooped beneath the folds of his cape, while a smile remained in precarious ascendancy over a grimace of pain. The power of the President's mind had also declined in the months since Teheran. Never a man who delighted in arduous intellectual combat or prolonged attention to detail, he now seemed more reluctant than ever to engage in argument. Impatient and weary, he seemed eager to patch together quick agreements and hasten the conference to its end. What impact, if any, the President's ill health had on the results of the Yalta conference is an extremely controversial question. Some of the President's defenders deny that his mind had lost its edge. The President knew exactly what he was doing, they say, and served the interests of his country well by negotiating the best agreements which could be obtained under the circumstances; where satisfactory agreements could not be obtained, he astutely arranged for decisions to be postponed. Many critics, on the other hand, charge that Stalin scored a great diplomatic victory over the non-Communist world because Roosevelt was too ill and too naive to resist. There is no way of knowing which interpretation is more valid, but in regard to the future of Germany it can be suggested that the President's lack of physical and mental energy at Yalta was more advantageous to the West than to Russia.

As an introduction to the discussion of the German question, Roosevelt said he hoped Stalin would repeat the toast offered at Teheran to the execution of 50,000 officers of the German army. "I am more bloodthirsty in regard to Germans than I was a year ago," the President said. "Everyone is more bloodthirsty now," Stalin replied, "for the Germans are savages who seem to hate the creative work of human beings with a sadistic hatred."[16] The President agreed. The next day in plenary session Stalin, doubtless feeling that he enjoyed the President's support, pressed for an immediate decision in favor of the dismemberment of Germany. Churchill, who had always looked on dismemberment with misgiving, played for time. Before a decision is made, said Churchill, there must be "elaborate searchings by experienced statesmen on the historical, political, economic and sociological aspects of the problem and prolonged study by a subcommittee."[17] We need not go into details now, answered Stalin, but we can reach a decision. No, said Churchill, there must be further study.

Roosevelt showed signs of impatience at the lengthy remarks of Churchill and Stalin. "I still think the division of Germany into five states or seven states is a good idea," the President said. "Or less," interjected Churchill, before launching into what appeared to be another long speech. At this point Secretary of State Edward R. Stettinius, Jr., who had formally replaced Hull after the 1944 elections, passed a note to the President. "We can readily agree to referring this—the 1st meeting of Foreign Ministers," it said. The President was grateful for the suggestion. Let us ask the Foreign Ministers to report on "the best method for the study of plans to dismember Germany," he said. [18] This was done.

Stettinius showed a greater readiness to support the British position in the meetings of foreign ministers than did Roosevelt in the plenary sessions. The result was a compromise formula by which the three Allies agreed to take such steps "including the complete disarmament, demilitarisation and the dismemberment of Germany *as they deem requisite for future peace and security.*"[19] The word "dismemberment" was included to meet the Russian demand, but the qualifying phrase, here given in italics, meant that no one was committed to anything. A com-

---

[16] *Ibid.*, p. 571. I have altered the indirect form of the minutes to first person discourse.

[17] *Ibid.*, p. 612.

[18] *Ibid.*, p. 614. For a facsimile of Stettinius's note to Roosevelt, see his *Roosevelt and the Russians: The Yalta Conference*, edited by Walter Johnson (Garden City, N. Y.: Doubleday, 1949), p. 125.

[19] *Foreign Relations, Yalta*, p. 978. Italics added.

mittee was established in London to study procedure for dismemberment. Thus, British wishes were met. President Roosevelt seemed to favor a decision on dismemberment at the conference itself, but the stubborn and interminable resistance of the British stood in the way. A weary President took the easier road to postponement. Possibly if his health and energy had allowed he would have made a greater effort to fight through to a decision with results that would have been even less satisfactory for the West.

The President's weariness may also have been a significant factor in his acquiescence in the French demand for a zone of occupation in Germany. At Teheran, it will be recalled, Roosevelt had spoken of France in words of unmitigated contempt. France, he believed at that time, had forfeited the right to a position of postwar power, should be deprived of her colonies, and prevented from rearming for the foreseeable future. But since Teheran France had been liberated and General de Gaulle had confounded Roosevelt's expectations by winning the support of an overwhelming majority of the French people. During most of 1944 Roosevelt, unreasonably influenced by his personal antipathy to de Gaulle, had refused to extend formal recognition to the General as head of the provisional government of France. The President persisted in his belief that recognition of de Gaulle by the United States would abet a plot to fasten a dictatorship on the French people against their will and thereby hasten the revolution which was to engulf the country after the war. At the same time the President suspected that Churchill's interest in seeing France restored as a military power was part of the Prime Minister's misguided infatuation with the discredited principle of the European balance of power. Events finally forced the President's hand. General Eisenhower, as Supreme Allied Commander, had to deal with someone in the civil administration of liberated France. De Gaulle had the authority and the organization; there was no one else with whom Eisenhower could work. Belatedly, in October 1944, the United States recognized what it could no longer deny: de Gaulle, for the time being at least, was the government of France.

De Gaulle, indignant that recognition had come so late, pressed on with that unrelenting devotion to the single ideal of French national prestige which became so familiar in later decades. He demanded and gained membership for France in the European Advisory Commission, he insisted in being invited to the next Big Three conference but was not, he declared that France must have its zone of occupation in Germany, and in December 1944 he went to Moscow and signed a treaty of mutual assistance with Stalin. Churchill meanwhile was encouraging de Gaulle's aspirations not because he found the General a comfortable ally, but because the impending departure of American power from Europe made the reconstruction of France a necessity.

Roosevelt was not happy with de Gaulle's success, but by the autumn of 1944 there was little he could do to stem it. After Hull's departure from the cabinet, the President had no adviser who shared his anti-French prejudices. On the contrary, a State Department "Briefing Book" memorandum prepared for his guidance at Yalta declared that the United States ought to help France regain her strength and influence in the interests of winning the war and preserving the peace. "It is likewise in the interest of this Government to treat France in all respects on the basis of her potential power and influence rather than on the basis of her present strength."[20] Worn down by the weight of advice at home and constant pleading from Churchill, Roosevelt in January 1945 decided to support the French bid for a zone of occupation. Hopefully he reasoned that de Gaulle might become easier to handle if appeased on this issue. Stalin at Yalta resisted the idea of a French zone and French membership on the Control Council for Germany, but he finally agreed after having won concessions on many other points. The French zone, shaped like an hourglass in the valley of the Rhine, was carved from the original American and to a lesser extent British zones. France also gained a sector in Berlin. The question of formal access rights to the city through the Soviet zone was again deferred. Assuming that these rights could be taken for granted, American planners thought that local commanders could work out all necessary arrangements.

Reparations took up much time at Yalta and touched the

---

[20] *Ibid.,* p. 300.

heart of the different ideas held by the three powers concerning Germany's future. Here the Russians aggressively seized the initiative by demanding that Germany be stripped of $20 billion worth of reparations, with half going to the Soviet Union. Reparations would take the form of heavy industrial equipment (the Russians suggested that 80 per cent of Germany's machinery ought to be removed), commodities, and forced labor. Here was a Morgenthau plan with a vengeance. The British would have none of it. They said that it was impossible to fix a dollar amount and that $20 billion was outrageously high. Germany would have to retain sufficient resources to keep the populace alive. Roosevelt and his advisers encountered great difficulty in devising American policy. Remembering the fiasco of reparations and war debts following the First World War, they were determined to avoid the situation where the United States again ended up paying any part of the bill. Thus, they insisted that any assessment must be within Germany's means. On the other hand, they did not want to give the impression to the Russians that the United States was lining up with Great Britain to prevent Russia from gaining compensation for the terrible suffering endured at German hands. Again, postponement for further study was the better part of wisdom. An arrangement was made for a three-power reparations commission to sit in Moscow and take $20 billion (half for Russia) "as a basis for discussion." The British resisted to the end the naming of any figure but were outvoted. It was agreed that reparations would consist of removal of property, annual delivery of goods from current production, and forced labor. The reparations commission did not meet until after Germany's defeat and was ultimately unable to reach any mutually acceptable agreements.

The Yalta accords on Germany were shadowy and incomplete. Concrete decisions could still be deferred, for the heart of the country including Berlin was still in German hands. Agreement could be made to appear more substantial than it actually was because policies had not yet had a chance to conflict in practice. But as Roosevelt returned from Washington, the potential shape of postwar Europe bore slight resemblance to what he had envisioned during 1943 and 1944. The last chance for a decision in favor of dismemberment had passed by. The Morgenthau plan had been tacitly renounced by Britain and the United States, although some of its flavor still lingered in the directive known as JCS [for Joint Chiefs of Staff] 1067 which was soon to be issued as a guide for American occupation policy. Assistant Secretary of War John J. McCloy, a leading architect of a moderate and constructive policy toward Germany, concluded JCS 1067 was "'harsh enough to win Russian support and yet moderate enough to prevent total chaos in Central Europe.''[21] More important, the directive was considered temporary. Policy could and did shift to meet changing circumstances, and throughout the spring of 1945 McCloy, Stimson, and planners in the State Department labored to see that it shifted in the direction of moderation. Morgenthau continued to fight a rearguard action in behalf of his ideas, but without success. In July 1945 he resigned when President Truman refused to take him to the Potsdam conference.

Even Roosevelt in his final days of life began to realize that policy toward Germany might have to take account of Soviet hostility. He rejected to the end the frantic insistence of Churchill that a showdown with Russia be faced while the West still had the millitary power to reinforce its diplomatic opinions, but his confidence was shaken by the ruthless character of Russian behavior throughout eastern and central Europe. His confidence in Stalin had reached a peak at Teheran and then continued on a slightly descending plateau through the Yalta conference. In April 1945 that plateau seemed about to fall off into a chasm of disillusionment.

---

[21] John L. Snell, *Wartime Origins of the East-West Dilemma Over Germany* (New Orleans: Hauser, 1959), p. 180.

CHAPTER VIII

The Fate of Poland

P RESIDENT ROOSEVELT'S assumptions about the possibilities of happy cooperation with Russia in the establishment of a peaceful and democratic world were subjected to greater strain by Soviet policy toward Poland than by any other wartime issue. The fate of Poland symbolized the collapse of the dream of Allied unity and the beginning of decades of open and ominous conflict between Russia and the West. Roosevelt and his advisers made every possible concession to Soviet views on Poland and hoped until the end that a genuine agreement could be reached. They failed and so did President Harry S. Truman in that brief interval before he decided in anger that Russia could no longer be treated as a trustworthy friend.

For many reasons the American government wished to avoid entanglement in the bitter quarrel between Moscow and the Polish government-in-exile in London. It seemed absolute folly to jeopardize victory over Germany, the chance of Russian entry into the war against Japan, and the dream of postwar unity by raising a difficult issue. Furthermore, it was far from clear in Washington whether Russia or Poland had the stronger case. Was the Soviet demand for the Curzon boundary line so unreasonable? And was it not fair for Moscow to insist on a Polish government composed of "friendly" individuals rather than stubborn foes of Russia and the Communist system? The President was also obsessed by the fear that millions of Polish Americans might vote against him in the 1944 election if a controversy over Poland erupted and he was forced to support the Russian position in public. Finally, there was the heavy weight of the tradition against American involvement in European political questions. Roosevelt, underestimating the readiness of the American people to assume permanent postwar responsibility, believed it was unwise to take a position which the public would not allow him to back up with something stronger than words. Indeed, the President—himself the product of isolationist decades—personally was dubious of the wisdom of American intervention in European politics regardless of what public opinion had to say on the subject.

At Teheran at the end of 1943, Roosevelt had conveyed the impression to Stalin that he agreed with Russian ideas on Poland but could not openly endorse them for domestic political reasons. He adhered to this position throughout notwithstanding increasing evidence that Soviet intentions in Poland were a travesty of Western concepts of political freedom and national independence. Polish Prime Minister Stanislaw Mikolajczyk, replacing Wladyslaw Sikorski who was killed in an airplane accident in July 1943, was tireless in his efforts to win British and American support against Russia. It was a frustrating task. Churchill tried to convince Mikolajczyk that Poland should accept the Curzon line and agree to remove some of the more extreme anti-Soviet members from the London government-in-exile. Mikolajczyk replied that he was willing to discuss the boundary but could make no final decisions before the war was over. He refused to allow the Soviets to dictate the membership of his cabinet. In June 1944 the Polish Prime Minister, after being put off several times, received an invitation to visit Roosevelt in Washington. The President was his usual affable self and characteristically implied that the United States was a more reliable friend to Poland than Britain. Mikolajczyk left Washington in improved spirits but without a shred of substantive support.

Meanwhile, the Red Army had advanced beyond the Curzon line and was nearing the outskirts of Warsaw. The Soviet government, having broken diplomatic relations with the Polish government in London in the spring of 1943 because of the controversy over the Katyn forest massacre, announced that the civil administration of liberated Poland was in the hands of the Committee of National Liberation with headquarters in

POLAND AFTER YALTA

Lublin. Thus, in mid-summer 1944 it appeared that Moscow was bent on ignoring the London Poles altogether. Mikolajczyk in desperation and in response to pressure from Churchill and Roosevelt went to Moscow at the end of July in a futile effort to make peace with Stalin. On the day following his arrival there began the most heart-rending single episode of Polish-Soviet wartime relations, the Warsaw uprising. The Polish underground inside Warsaw gave its allegiance to the government-in-exile in London, but nevertheless was jubilant at the approach of the liberating Red Army which by July 31 had reached within twelve miles of the city. Encouraged by radio broadcasts from Moscow, the people of Warsaw on that day attacked the German troops in the city. Believing that Russian divisions would be in Warsaw in a matter of days, the Polish patriots faced German tanks, machine guns, and planes almost without armament of their own. But the Russian advance stopped the moment the uprising began. For two months the lines remained static outside the city while the Germans proceeded to annihilate tens of thousands of underground fighters who happened to be potential political rivals to the puppet Lublin committee then waiting safely behind Soviet lines. The Russians claimed that their long pause outside Warsaw was justified on tactical grounds. Whether or not the claim was true, tactics also served to control the political future of Poland in Russia's favor.

The leaders of the uprising sent poignant pleas for help, but Stalin refused to act. The uprising, he said, is the work of criminals and irresponsible agitators. Churchill, however, was determined to do everything possible for the valiant Poles. He urged Roosevelt to join him in strong protests to Stalin. The President was loath to become involved but he did associate himself with a mildly worded request to Stalin that British and American planes from Italy be allowed to land behind Soviet lines after dropping arms to the Poles in Warsaw. Stalin replied with a brutal refusal. "I do not see what further steps we can take at the present time," said Roosevelt to Churchill. The Prime Minister was not to be denied so easily. He proposed to Roosevelt that a stronger appeal be sent to Stalin and then, if Stalin still refused to cooperate, that planes be sent to land behind Soviet lines without permission. The President rejected this scheme and invoked the need to have Soviet support against Japan. Churchill could not act without American agreement, but in recalling the moment in after years he said he would have liked to have told Stalin, "We are sending our aeroplanes to land in your territory after delivering supplies to Warsaw. If you do not treat them properly all convoys will be stopped from this moment by us." By now time was fast running out in Warsaw. Frantically, Churchill continued to seek Roosevelt's support, sending three long telegrams on September 4 alone. The President, however, had been incorrectly informed that the uprising was over (actually resistance continued until October 2). With a sense of sorrow and relief that procrastination had removed a problem, he again replied to Churchill that "there now appears to be nothing we can do."[1]

In addition to their desire for eventual Soviet help against Japan, Roosevelt and his advisers in Washington were reluctant to irritate Russia over Poland because of their intense wish for Russian cooperation in laying the foundations of a postwar world security organization. At Dumbarton Oaks, an estate on the outskirts of Washington, representatives of Britain, Russia, and the United States were then deep in conference on that question. To the dedicated disciples of Secretary of State Hull it seemed that the success of the Dumbarton Oaks conference would create the means for settling all such problems as Polish-Soviet discord. On the other hand, the failure of Dumbarton Oaks would be the end to all hopes for lasting peace. Many British diplomats and some Americans believed that enthusiasm in Washington for the potential of a world organization was excessive and was unfortunately diverting attention from pressing practical problems. For example, George F. Kennan, then counselor of the American embassy in Moscow and later the foremost historian of Soviet-American relations, warned:

An international organization for the preservation of peace and security cannot take the place of a well-conceived and realistic foreign policy . . . and we are being . . . negligent of the interests of our people if we allow plans for an international organization to be an excuse for failing to occupy ourselves seriously and minutely with the sheer power relationships of the European peoples.[2]

Roosevelt, however, was determined to occupy himself as little as possible with those power relationships until after the election. Not so Prime Minister Churchill. Seeing that all of

---

[1] Winston S. Churchill, *Triumph and Tragedy* (Boston: Houghton Mifflin, 1953), pp. 139–144.

[2] Quoted by Herbert Feis, *Churchill, Roosevelt, Stalin: The War They Waged and the Peace They Sought* (Princeton, N. J.: Princeton University Press, 1957), p. 436.

Poland would soon be in Soviet hands, he flew to Moscow in October 1944 in a further attempt to bring about an accommodation between Poles and Russians. Ambassador Averell Harriman stood by as an observer, not a participant, and thereby symbolized Roosevelt's detachment. Representatives of the puppet Lublin committee and Prime Minister Mikolajczyk joined in these lengthy Moscow conversations but no progress was made. In November Mikolajczyk, despondent over the feebleness of British and American support and under criticism from right-wing associates for having gone to Moscow, resigned and was replaced by Miroslaw Arciszewski. The reorganized Polish cabinet was more rigidly anti-Soviet than the old. As the year 1944 came to an end the deadlock over Poland seemed more hopeless than ever. The Polish government in London refused to accept the Curzon line as a boundary and Stalin just as adamantly refused to consider any other. Power lay with Russia, for Churchill publicly and Roosevelt privately were supporting the Curzon line, or something close to it, as a fair boundary. The one chance for an independent Poland appeared to be the formation of a representative government combining members of the London group, the Lublin committee, and other leaders from inside Poland. But neither the Poles in London nor the Soviets, speaking through the Lublin committee, were willing to consider any solution which gave a share of real power to the other side. Few Americans appreciated how slight were the chances for arriving at a settlement satsifactory to all concerned.

Although Poland was the primary purpose of Churchill's trip to Moscow, he was also anxious to reach a temporary accord with Stalin on a division of Anglo-Soviet responsibility in southeastern Europe—a region where President Roosevelt had many times disclaimed all desire for American political involvement. At that time Soviet troops controlled Rumania and Bulgaria and had nearly completed the occupation of Hungary. The Germans were in retreat from Greece and near the end of their power in Yugoslavia. All five countries were plagued by lethal internal discord. Churchill realized that stability would have to be imposed by the liberating powers. Russia had already liberated Rumania and Bulgaria. But what of Greece where the British were engaged in a desperate effort to support moderate and conservative elements against Greek Communists? And what of Yugoslavia where Churchill was trying to create a workable accord between Tito's powerful partisan forces and the Yugoslavian government-in-exile in London? Would Stalin intervene to upset British aims? Realistically, Churchill concluded that an agreement on spheres of influence was essential. During the previous summer he had received a disapproving response from Secretary of State Hull to this idea, but now in Moscow he had Roosevelt's vague approval. Accordingly, in a scene which his own memoirs have made famous, the Prime Minister jotted down a proposed country-by-country division of "predominance": Rumania—90 per cent for Russia and 10 per cent for the others; Greece—90 per cent for Great Britain "(in accord with U.S.A.)" and 10 per cent for Russia; Yugoslavia and Bulgaria—50–50 per cent; Rumania—75 per cent for Russia and 25 per cent for the others. In Churchill's words:

> After this there was a long silence. The pencilled paper lay in the centre of the table. At length I said, "Might it not be thought rather cynical if it seemed we had disposed of these issues, so fateful to millions of people, in such an offhand manner? Let us burn the paper." "No, you keep it," said Stalin.[3]

Poland was not included in this informal accord, but the virtual free hand which Churchill secured to suppress Greek Communists by force made it difficult for him to protest against Russian intervention in Polish internal affairs. The spheres of predominance agreement also added to the suspicions which many Americans already had of British tactics in Europe. The agreement seemed to symbolize the worst aspects of international rivalry in the evil days of the balance of power; it confirmed the inclination of many American diplomats to distrust British advice when seeking a solution to European problems.

After his election victory Roosevelt began to give more attention to Poland. In November 1944 he urged Stalin to allow Poland to keep the important city of Lwow and the surrounding oil fields although they were located on the Soviet side of the

---

[3] Churchill, *Triumph and Tragedy*, pp. 227–228.

Curzon line. Stalin was unreceptive. Details of the frontier settlement, however, were far less important than the question of who would rule Poland after the war: successors to the London government-in-exile, the Lublin group, or some combination of various elements. And how would the postwar government be selected? By free elections with a genuine choice of candidates and without intimidation of the voters? Or by Soviet-style elections with a single slate of candidates and the use of terror as a main ingredient in the political process? The reports which Ambassador Harriman was sending from Moscow at the end of the year were not optimistic. The Soviets, he said, appear bent on the domination of internal Polish affairs. Any Pole who would not accept Soviet policies would be conveniently branded a "Fascist." In short, the Soviet concept of the terms "friendly" and "independent" as applied to Poland and other neighboring states, warned Harriman, appears "to mean something quite different from our interpretation."[4]

At the same time it appeared that Moscow was on the verge of recognizing the Lublin committee as the government of Poland, thus further closing the door on the London government-in-exile which was still recognized, although without enthusiasm, by the United States and Britain. But the President remained confident that these apparent difficulties would dissolve the moment he again met Stalin face to face. In the middle of December he appealed to Stalin not to recognize the Lublin committee before their meeting "which I hope will be immediately after my inauguration of January 20."[5] Stalin replied with a denunciation of alleged criminal terrorist activity by agents of the Polish government-in-exile operating in Poland. He said he had no reason to delay recognition of the Lublin committee. Roosevelt answered, in a telegram prepared for his signature by the Department of State, that he was "disturbed and deeply disappointed" by Stalin's statement but still hoped Russia would postpone recognition of a group which obviously did not represent the people of Poland.

---

[4] Telegram of December 28, 1944, U. S. Department of State, *Foreign Relations, The Conferences at Malta and Yalta, 1945* (Washington: U. S. Government Printing Office, 1955), p. 65.

[5] *Ibid.*, p. 218.

I cannot ignore the fact that up to the present only a small fraction of Poland proper west of the Curzon Line has been liberated from German tyranny, and it is therefore an unquestioned truth that the people of Poland have had no opportunity to express themselves in regard to the Lublin Committee.[6]

Seldom before had the President spoken so bluntly, but Stalin was unmoved. The Soviets recognized the Lublin committee on December 31 as the provisional government of Poland. Thus, when Roosevelt and Churchill arrived at Yalta they confronted a *fait accompli*. Meanwhile, according to a report from Harriman which was brought specially to the President's attention on January 12, 1945, the Soviets in Poland and throughout eastern Europe were

employing the wide variety of means at their disposal — occupation troops, secret police, local communist parties, labor unions, sympathetic leftist organizations, sponsored cultural societies, and economic pressure — to assure the establishment of regimes which . . . actually depend for their existence on groups responsive to all suggestions emanating from the Kremlin.[7]

The State Department, whose role in the formulation of policy was slowly beginning to expand since the resignation of Secretary of State Hull, prepared a detailed analysis of desirable objectives in Poland for the use of the American delegation at Yalta. In seeking a truly democratic and independent Poland, the Department said, "we should endeavor to prevent any interim regime from being established which would exclude any major element of the population and threaten to crystallize into a permanent government before the will of the population could become manifest." Specifically, the United States should resist the growth of power by "the so-called provisional government at Lublin" which seemed to owe its existence largely to the Red Army and the NKVD, the Soviet secret police. For the future the United States should insist on free elections under

---

[6] Sent December 30, 1944, *ibid.*, p. 224.
[7] *Ibid.*, p. 450.

effective supervision. In regard to boundaries the Department suggested the Curzon line plus Lwow and the oil fields on the east, but warned against the Soviet plan to place Poland's other boundary far to the west at Germany's expense.

By including a large section of German territory in Poland and the probable transfer of some eight to ten million Germans, the future Polish state would in all probability be forced to depend completely on Moscow for protection against German Irredentists' demands and in fact might become a full-fledged Soviet satellite.[8]

It was one thing to describe American aims for Poland, but quite another to find effective means for achieving them against Soviet determination to create a puppet state with a Communist government. Obviously, the Soviet will could be bent, if at all, only by hard bargaining, a readiness to apply pressure by withholding favors, and a willingness to do without Soviet assistance in some other areas. President Roosevelt was prepared to do none of these things. Above all he did not want to annoy the Soviets over an issue like Poland when his military advisers said that Russia's participation in the war against Japan was necessary to save untold thousands of American lives. Nothing could take priority over the need to pin Stalin down to his earlier promise in that regard. Furthermore, the President's temperament, health, and assumptions about how to handle Stalin all made him avoid prolonged and stubborn negotiations. Similarly, his fear of arousing Soviet suspicions prevented him and many of his advisers from giving serious consideration to sanctions in the form of a reduction or suspension of American aid. On the contrary, Secretary of the Treasury Morgenthau was urging in January 1945 that the United States offer Russia a $10 billion low-interest loan (as compared with $6 billion for which the Soviet government had asked and $6.5 billion tentatively promised to Great Britain). Ignoring the recommendation of State Department officials that economic aid to Russia should be used as a diplomatic bargaining tool, Morgenthau argued that a generous "gesture on our part would reassure the Soviet Government of our determination to cooperate with them and break down any suspicions the Soviet authorities might have

---

[8] *Ibid.*, pp. 230–232.

in regard to our future action." He also suggested to Roosevelt that the "credit to Russia would be a major step in your program to provide 60 million jobs in the post-war period."[9] Although negotiations for a loan ultimately collapsed, the Secretary of the Treasury's proposal is important as an indication of the currents of thought swirling around the President.

In addition a strong American stand on Poland continued to be inhibited by the desire to commit Russia unequivocally to the world security organization. Although the Dumbarton Oaks conference had been hailed as a great success, one crucial and several lesser but still important issues had not been decided. If these issues could not be solved at Yalta, there might never be a world security organization. The implicit connection between the American dream of a world organization and the problem of Soviet behavior in Poland illustrates the presence at Yalta of two conflicting concepts of national security. The world organization, according to the American ideal, would enable all nations large and small to live without fear of attack. There would be no need for any nation to impose its will on weaker neighbors in order to build walls against potential enemies, as Russia seemed to be doing in Poland. The only way to persuade Russia to abandon her old-fashioned concepts, Americans argued, was to demonstrate that the new system could become a reality. On the other hand, direct criticism and opposition to Russian plans in Poland would confirm the Soviets in their suspicions and thus defeat the basic American purpose. This circle of precarious "ifs" was completed by Secretary of State Stettinius's fear that the American people would reject membership in the world organization, as they had done in 1919, if Russia refused to permit genuine independence for Poland.

The crucial question about the world organization concerned the extent of the veto power by the permanent members of the security council. The Russians, fearing that the world might combine against them, at first insisted on an absolute veto power even over whether or not a question would be discussed. The Americans argued that such a device would make the organiza-

---

[9] *Ibid.*, pp. 315, 321.

tion unacceptable to all smaller nations. After long discussion an ambiguous compromise was devised and accepted. The simple discussion of an issue in the council was not subject to a veto. Furthermore, the great powers would abstain from voting on council recommendations for peaceful settlement of disputes to which they were a party. The veto did apply, however, on all council votes for action (as contrasted with recommendations for peaceful settlement) whether or not the vetoing power was a party to the dispute in question. This formula reflected the determination of President Roosevelt and many other Americans that the world organization must not be able to compel the United States to use its armed forces without its specific consent.

After the Russians suddenly' accepted this formula midway in the conference, the lesser issues were settled quickly. Russia was granted three votes in the assembly of the organization after having asked for sixteen votes during the Dumbarton Oaks conference. In order to protect himself against possible public outcry concerning these three votes the President secured British and Russian agreement to support an American demand for three votes should it prove necessary. The Big Three also agreed that San Francisco would be the location for the meeting to draft the charter of the organization, that the meeting would begin on April 25, 1945, and that only those states which had declared war on Germany would be invited. Churchill's fears that the world organization might meddle with British colonialism were allayed by an agreement that trusteeship status would apply only to former League of Nations mandates, territory detached from the enemy, and areas placed voluntarily under trusteeship by the governing power. These agreements were received by the American delegation with rejoicing. Like the faith of Woodrow Wilson in his League of Nations in the previous generation, their faith in the world organization enabled them to accept compromise agreements on issues such as Poland.

The Yalta agreement on Poland was a tissue of words over a chasm of still unresolved difference. The only point firmly nailed down concerned the Polish-Soviet border. Roosevelt repeated his suggestion that Russia allow Poland to retain Lwow and the oil fields, as a magnanimous gesture, but did not insist upon it. Stalin was unmoved. The boundary was drawn along the Curzon line with very slight deviations in Poland's favor. Lwow and the oil fields became Russian territory. The Russians pressed for a Polish-German boundary along the Oder and western Neisse rivers. Roosevelt and Churchill agreed that Poland should receive some compensation at Germany's expense, but the Oder-Neisse line was excessive. "It would be a pity," said Churchill, "to stuff the Polish goose so full of German food that it died of indigestion."[10] After hours of discussion it was finally decided to postpone the western boundary settlement until the Poles themselves could be consulted. To anticipate, Britain and the United States never did agree formally to the Oder-Neisse line, but the Russians achieved their aim by simply deporting the Germans from the disputed area and turning the territory over to Poland.

The most important and controversial aspect of the agreement on Poland dealt with the character of the new Polish government. The Russians proposed that the Lublin committee, which they recognized as the provisional government, be enlarged by the addition of "some democratic leaders from Polish émigré circles" and then recognized by Britain and the United States.[11] This government should then hold elections as soon as possible for the formation of a permanent government. The British and Americans objected to the word "émigré" to describe the London Poles and balked also at the dominant role assigned by Stalin to the Lublin committee. The Anglo-American preference was for a completely reorganized interim government, in which Lublin Poles would play a minor role, followed by free elections under effective supervision. The Russians argued back that the government they recognized was fully representative and was already functioning. Supervised elections, the Russians said, were an insult to Polish independence. The British and Americans, anxious for agreement, gave in. The resulting three-power agreement was sufficiently ambiguous to be hailed as a triumph for Polish independence and sufficiently weak to allow the Russians to exercise a free hand while claiming that they were not violating their pledged word. The Russians won their main objective: the new government was to be formed by the

---

[10] *Ibid.*, pp. 717, 725.
[11] *Ibid.*, p. 716.

reorganization of "the Provisional Government which is now functioning in Poland." The British and American ambassadors in Moscow were to consult with Molotov and various Poles for this purpose. The reorganized government was to be accorded diplomatic recognition by the three great powers and was to hold free (but unsupervised) elections as soon as possible. All "democratic and anti-Nazi parties" could participate in the elections.[12] The words were idealistic, but the connotation was ominous given Stalin's opinion that most of the Poles associated with the London government-in-exile were akin to Nazis.

Roosevelt and his advisers at Yalta showed far less concern over developments in southeastern Europe than they did for Poland. Three of these countries—Hungary, Rumania, and Bulgaria—were Axis satellites. Greece was Britian's concern and Yugoslavia, now dominated by the personality of Tito, seemed primarily a question for Anglo-Soviet discussion. Compared with Poland, these countries had sent few immigrants to the United States, therefore, Roosevelt felt little domestic political pressure to act on their behalf. Furthermore, their location was remote and their internal politics too hideously confused for most Americans to understand. It appeared futile and unwise for the American government to intervene directly in the affairs of these countries, especially when Russia and Britain (in Greece and to a lesser degree in Yugoslavia) were already on the scene. If larger issues, such as the fate of Germany, the future of Poland, and the establishment of a world security organization, were satisfactorily worked out, it seemed likely that these smaller countries would develop toward democracy and freedom. But if the great powers could not cooperate on the major issues, what use was there in attempting to set detailed ground rules for less important areas, especially areas where long tradition proclaimed that the United States had no business getting politically involved?

Some American observers argued against this line of reasoning and claimed that the nature of the peace would depend on what happened in numerous areas which individually did not seem particularly important. The United States, they said, must break completely with the old tradition of nonentanglement and

---

[12] *Ibid.*, p. 980.

show a sustained concern for what happened everywhere in Europe. Even while the Yalta conference was in session, they warned that most of eastern Europe was on the verge of being turned into a totalitarian extension of the Soviet Communist system. The one exception was Greece, but to some Americans it seemed that Britain's forcible suppression of Communist elements in Greece was as bad as or worse than whatever the Soviets were supposedly doing in Hungary, Rumania, Bulgaria and elsewhere. The United States met this situation with a proposal that the three great powers proclaim their good intentions in the form of a "Declaration on Liberated Europe." Russia and Britain readily agreed. By this document, which should be read in conjunction with the accord on Poland, the three governments agreed to cooperate in helping the peoples of liberated Europe and the former Nazi satellites "to form interim governmental authorities broadly representative of all democratic elements in the population and pledged to the earliest possible establishment through free elections of governments responsive to the will of the people." The three governments further agreed to consult each other immediately "on the measures necessary to discharge [their] joint responsibilities" and then concluded with a rhapsody of idealism:

By this declaration we reaffirm our faith in the principles of the Atlantic Charter, our pledge in the declaration by the United Nations, and our determination to build in cooperation with other peace-loving nations world order under law, dedicated to peace, security, freedom and general well-being of all mankind.[13]

The Americans at Yalta had no desire to poke too hard at these tender words. They believed that time was on the side of freedom. The success of each agreement signed at the conference would strengthen the others. Past discord would be ignored in the mutual triumph over Germany and Japan. Russian cooperation would mean a healthy birth for the world organization at San Francisco and the rapid and final defeat of the Axis. Having no further reasons to feel insecure, Russia would then join in the reconstruction of a democratic Europe. And the American people, seeing their ideals fulfilled around the world, would embrace the organization born at San Francisco. The vision of

---

[13] *Ibid.*, p. 977–978.

Woodrow Wilson would be achieved and his forlorn ghost laid to rest. "We really believed in our hearts that this was the dawn of a new day," said Harry Hopkins who was at Yalta but too ill to sit at the conference table. "We were absolutely certain that we had won the first great victory of the peace—and, by 'we,' I mean *all* of us, the whole civilized human race."[14]

This optimism lasted a few weeks longer, notwithstanding a flood of evidence that Russia had no intention of following the Anglo-American interpretation of the Yalta agreement on Poland. Early in March Harriman in Moscow reported that the Soviets were placing shocking obstructions in the way of calling representative Poles together in order to form a new government. Meanwhile, no Westerner could tell what was happening inside Poland because Russia would not allow observers into the country. Tales of intimidation and mass political arrests, however, were plentiful. It was in this atmosphere that Secretary of State Stettinius told the cabinet in Washington on March 13 that the successful meeting at Yalta demonstrated "the Russian desire to cooperate along all lines with" the United States.[15] On the same day Churchill cabled Roosevelt: "Poland has lost her frontier. Is she now to lose her freedom? . . . [W]e are in presence of a great failure and an utter breakdown of what was settled at Yalta." British strength, he said, was insufficient to move the Soviets; "combined dogged pressure" was necessary.[16] The President reacted negatively and denied that a breakdown of the Yalta agreement had occurred. Significantly, he emphasized in a cabinet meeting three days later that he was having difficulty with the British, not the Russians. "In a semi-jocular manner of speaking, he stated that the British were perfectly willing for the United States to have a war with Russia at any time and that, in his opinion, to follow the British program would be to proceed toward that end."[17]

---

[14] Robert E. Sherwood, *Roosevelt and Hopkins: An Intimate History* (New York: Harper, 1948), p. 870.

[15] Walter Millis (Ed.), *The Forrestal Diaries*, (New York: Viking, 1951), p. 35.

[16] Churchill, *Triumph and Tragedy*, p. 426.

[17] Memorandum by the Assistant Secretary of the Navy, who attended the meeting, *Forrestal Diaries*, pp. 36–37.

President Roosevelt may have been preparing to alter his attitude toward Russia during the final weeks of his life, but the evidence is too fragmentary to support a firm conclusion. The President was disturbed by Stalin's unwillingness to send Foreign Secretary Molotov to the approaching San Francisco conference for the founding of the world security organization. He was deeply pained by Soviet accusations of Anglo-American perfidy in the abortive negotiations for the surrender of the German armies in Italy. He also admonished Stalin over Poland and admitted to Churchill on April 11 that we "shall have to consider most carefully the implications of Stalin's attitude and what is to be our next step." And yet on the day he died (April 12) the President sent Stalin a friendly message and cabled to Churchill, "I would minimise the Soviet problem as much as possible, because these problems, in one form or another, seem to arise every day, and most of them straighten out. . . ."[18] If a new realism toward Russia was grappling with the old assumptions within the mind of the President on that soft spring day, the old assumptions were still on top.

In relation to the tasks confronting him, no man was ever less prepared to assume the Presidency than Harry S. Truman. After an ordinary career in domestic politics and without the slightest briefing from Roosevelt, he knew little more about problems of foreign policy than any intelligent reader of the newspapers. But he possessed great assets in his readiness to seek and take advice, in his blunt courage and combative common sense, and—above all—in his capacity for decision.

During his first weeks in office President Truman attempted to follow the broad lines of policy which Roosevelt had established. He lacked both the desire and the information to strike out in new directions, and he was surrounded by Roosevelt's closest advisers. Thus, he was encouraged by Stalin's an-

---

[18] Churchill, *Triumph and Tragedy*, pp. 439, 454.

nouncement that in tribute to Roosevelt's memory Molotov would attend the San Francisco conference after all. This gesture seemed to indicate that the Soviets truly intended to support a world organization. At the same time, Truman and his advisers resisted, just as Roosevelt had resisted, Churchill's pleas that Anglo-American troop dispositions be used as levers against Russia. The chance to capture Berlin before the Russians was passed by and American troops waited for several days close by Prague, capital of Czechoslovakia, in order that Soviet troops could occupy the city. And then, after the German surrender, troops under Eisenhower's command were quickly withdrawn westward to the original lines of zonal demarcation.

By relinquishing a band of German territory up to one hundred miles in depth, the United States was meeting its obligations with scrupulous care. Churchill, however, was downcast. He argued that the West should hold every possible acre on the grounds that the Soviets had already violated their obligations in Poland as well as in every other central and eastern European country except Greece where the British were dominant. The Russians were drawing "an iron curtain" across the continent, Churchill warned on May 12, and it was imperative to save as much of Europe as possible before the American armies were withdrawn.[19] In the eyes of most of Truman's advisers, Churchill's recommendation was utterly wrongheaded and dangerous. If followed it would destroy all the hopes for cooperation with Russia which were now associated with the cherished memory of President Roosevelt.

Meanwhile, President Truman accumulated information and began to form his own conclusions. The Polish question above all else caused him to doubt the possibility of easy cooperation with Russia. He was not ready to consider forcing a showdown, for his military advisers said Russia's entry into the war against Japan was still a necessity, but when Molotov passed through Washington on his way to San Francisco the President gave the Soviet Foreign Minister a stern lecture on Russian behavior in Poland. "I have never been talked to like that in my life," said Molotov, according to Truman's account. "Carry out your agree-

---

[19] *Ibid.*, pp. 572–574.

ments and you won't get talked to like that," Truman replied.[20]
The President's natural inclination was to be as tough with the
Russians as they were with him. In this he was supported by
Churchill, of course, and at home by Secretary of the Navy
Forrestal. But too much was at stake. He decided to suspend
judgment until he had a chance to meet Churchill and Stalin.

Events immediately preceding the last wartime Big Three conference, held in the Berlin suburb of Potsdam in July 1945,
seemed for the moment to support the validity of the old Rooseveltian assumptions and to discredit further the Churchillian
alternative. In preparation for this meeting Truman sent two
special emissaries to confer with Churchill and Stalin respec-
tively during the final week of May. Joseph E. Davies, famed for
his favorable and emotional attitude toward Russia, went to
London; and Harry Hopkins, near death and performing his last
overseas mission, went to Moscow. Davies berated Churchill
for harboring unwarranted suspicions of Russia. "Are you now
willing to declare," Davies asked, "that you and Britain were
wrong in not supporting Hitler who expressed a similar determination to oppose Russia?" Churchill showed admirable self-
control while listening to this tirade, but Davies told Truman
that the Prime Minister "was basically more concerned over
preserving England's position in Europe than in preserving
Peace." This attitude, said Davies, "could and does undoubtedly
account for much of the aggressiveness and so-called unilateral
action on the part of the Soviets since Yalta."[21]

At that moment Hopkins, who was in general agreement with
Davies's analysis and whose illness since the Teheran conference
had insulated him from the full impact of Soviet hostility, was
in Moscow conducting amiable conversations with Stalin. His
purpose was to convince the Soviet leader that the United States
was totally opposed to Churchill's anti-Russian policies, but
at the same time disturbed by the increasing difficulty of reach-

---

[20] Harry S. Truman, *Memoirs*, Vol. 1, *Year of Decisions (Garden City,*
N. Y.: Doubleday, 1955), p. 82. This and subsequent quotations from the
Truman *Memoirs* used with the permission of Time, Inc.

[21] *Foreign Relations, Conference of Berlin (Potsdam), 1945* (2 vols., 1960),
Vol. 1, pp. 73, 77. Hereafter cited as *Foreign Relations, Potsdam*. I have put
the paraphrase of Davies's report into direct statement.

ing agreement with the Soviets on a variety of issues. Specifically, Hopkins succeeded in ending an impasse which had developed at San Francisco over the ambiguous Yalta agreement on the veto power in the new world organization and also reached an agreement on which Poles, in addition to the puppet Lublin group, would be invited to Moscow in order to create the reorganized government envisioned at Yalta. Hopkins's first achievement led to the signing of the Charter of the United Nations on June 25, 1945. The Charter, said Truman to the delegates in San Francisco, "is a solid structure upon which we can build a better world. . . . Between the victory in Europe and the final victory in Japan, in this most destructive of all wars, you have won a victory against war itself."[22] Hopkins's second achievement led to the establishment of the Provisional Polish Government of National Unity on June 28. Two-thirds of this government consisted of Lublin Poles, but Mikolajczyk was second deputy prime minister. Within a week the London government-in-exile was liquidated and diplomatic recognition extended to the new government by the United States and Britain. Another tissue agreement had been pasted over the hard reality of Soviet political domination in Poland.

Thus matters stood on July 7 when President Truman boarded the cruiser *Augusta* for his trip to Europe and the Potsdam conference. Now that Germany was defeated, the United Nations established, and the Polish question quiet for the moment, his thoughts were dominated by two insistent questions concerning Asia. How soon and by what methods would Japan be defeated? Would Russia cooperate in the establishment of a unified China under the leadership of Chiang Kai-shek?

---

[22] Truman, *Memoirs*, Vol. 1, p. 289.

CHAPTER IX

The Bomb

O N AUGUST 6, 1945 Hiroshima was annihilated by an atomic bomb dropped from an American B-29. Japan surrendered within days. But even as they rejoiced, all thoughtful men trembled in the presence of victory's awful companion: the knowledge that the United States had perfected and demonstrated man's capacity to destroy the world. In after years the American conscience has been plagued by this cataclysmic deed. Was it necessary? Did responsible leaders consider the consequences of their act, and give adequate thought to withholding the bomb or demonstrating its power to Japan before it was used against humanity? The answers to these questions are infinite, for they depend on the individual's opinion of the extent to which leaders in time of crisis can transcend the limitations of old assumptions, incomplete information, overloaded administrative machinery, and fatigue. All that can be said with assurance is that the men who decided to drop the bomb acted conscientiously and with a sense of responsibility for mankind insofar as they were able. History may call this decision a tragic mistake, but can he who would condemn the decision makers as individuals say that he would have acted otherwise in the circumstances?

The first circumstance which must be kept in mind is that the secrecy, uncertainty, timing, and revolutionary character of the atomic project prevented the American government from using the bomb's potential as a factor in diplomatic and military calculations until the last three months of the war, and even then the calculations were sporadic and poorly coordinated. Knowledge of the bomb, notwithstanding the enormous size and number of installations required for its development, was restricted to a handful of scientists and a much smaller number of military and political leaders. For example, Admiral Leahy, the President's personal chief of staff, did not learn of the bomb until September 1944. (Commenting then as an expert on explosives, he said he doubted the thing would work.) The Secretary of State was not let in on the secret until January 1945, and until the day of Hiroshima so few men were aware of the bomb that it was impossible to use the knowledge of the new weapon at the lower and intermediate levels where military and political planning begins. Furthermore, even those scientists who were absolutely confident of the theoretical soundness of the bomb were not sure the device would explode under combat conditions. Until the very end the bomb was a long shot on which cautious men were unwilling to count too heavily. It always seemed wise to make calculations as if no bomb existed. If it worked, so much the better.

Timing also inhibited thorough high-level consideration of the bomb's implications. The first firm forecasts that an operational bomb would be ready in August 1945 were not made by the scientists until December 1944. From that time until his death, President Roosevelt was too occupied with the closing stages of the war in Europe and the myriad political problems with Russia to give sustained thought to the meaning of the bomb. Harry Truman knew nothing of the bomb before he became President and the problems competing for his attention were, if anything, more numerous and complex than those that Roosevelt had faced. Even if the time had been available, Roosevelt's mind was too fatigued and Truman's too busy to have comprehended the revolutionary nature of the problem mankind was about to confront. They understood on the purely verbal level that an explosive a thousand times more destructive than anything in existence would soon be ready. But in a war where thousand-bomber raids had already turned cities to infernoes and where tens of millions had died, such comparative figures had slight impact on the imagination. Many scientists comprehended the awesome nature of the bomb. They could communicate words to their military and political superiors, but not true understanding. It should be added that even the scientists per-

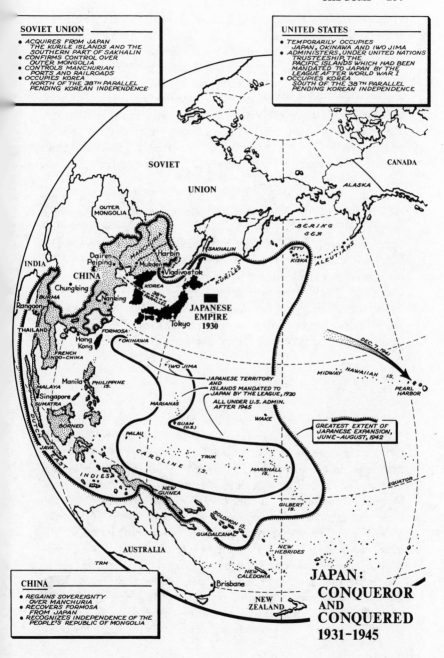

SOVIET UNION
- ACQUIRES FROM JAPAN THE KURILE ISLANDS AND THE SOUTHERN PART OF SAKHALIN
- CONFIRMS CONTROL OVER OUTER MONGOLIA
- CONTROLS MANCHURIAN PORTS AND RAILROADS
- OCCUPIES KOREA NORTH OF THE 38TH PARALLEL PENDING KOREAN INDEPENDENCE

UNITED STATES
- TEMPORARILY OCCUPIES JAPAN, OKINAWA AND IWO JIMA
- ADMINISTERS, UNDER UNITED NATIONS TRUSTEESHIP THE PACIFIC ISLANDS WHICH HAD BEEN MANDATED TO JAPAN BY THE LEAGUE AFTER WORLD WAR I
- OCCUPIES KOREA SOUTH OF THE 38TH PARALLEL PENDING KOREAN INDEPENDENCE

CHINA
- REGAINS SOVEREIGNTY OVER MANCHURIA
- RECOVERS FORMOSA FROM JAPAN
- RECOGNIZES INDEPENDENCE OF THE PEOPLE'S REPUBLIC OF MONGOLIA

SOVIET

UNION

CANADA

OUTER MONGOLIA

MANCHURIA

ALASKA

BERING SEA

Dairen
Peiping
Harbin
Mukden
Vladivostok

SAKHALIN

ATTU
KISKA

ALEUTIANS

INDIA

CHINA

Chungking

Nanking

KOREA
38TH PARALLEL

KURILES

Rangoon

BURMA

JAPANESE
EMPIRE
1930

Tokyo

THAILAND

FORMOSA

OKINAWA

Hong Kong

FRENCH INDO-CHINA

IWO JIMA

JAPANESE TERRITORY AND ISLANDS MANDATED TO JAPAN BY THE LEAGUE, 1920
ALL UNDER U.S. ADMIN. AFTER 1945

MIDWAY

HAWAIIAN IS.

DEC. 7, 1941

PEARL HARBOR

Manila

PHILIPPINE IS.

MALAYA

MARIANAS

WAKE

Singapore

SUMATRA

GUAM (U.S.)

BORNEO

PALAU

GREATEST EXTENT OF JAPANESE EXPANSION, JUNE-AUGUST, 1942

DUTCH

CAROLINE IS.

TRUK

MARSHALL IS.

JAVA

EAST

INDIES

NEW GUINEA

GILBERT IS.

EQUATOR

SOLOMON IS.

GUADALCANAL

NEW HEBRIDES

AUSTRALIA

TRM

NEW CALEDONIA

Brisbane

NEW ZEALAND

**JAPAN:
CONQUEROR
AND
CONQUERED
1931–1945**

sistently underestimated the bomb's explosive power, although not its potential for almost limitless future development. The December 1944 estimates envisioned a device equal to 500 tons of TNT. The bolder guessers had increased this to 5000 tons on the eve of the first test at Alamogordo, but even this estimate was vastly exceeded. The Hiroshima bomb was equal to 20,000 tons of TNT. More important, the scientists vastly underrated the dangers of radioactivity. An informed estimate on the eve of Hiroshima was that the radioactive danger zone would not extend more than two thirds of a mile from the point of explosion.

Finally, the momentum of policies developed over a long period of time on the basis of assumptions unrelated to the bomb was too great to allow men to pause long enough to assimilate the new factor. Even if men had been able to ask specifically how, for example, the bomb ought to alter American policy toward Asia, events were moving so fast that one day's answer would be obsolete the next. Thus, through the first months of 1945, American plans for Asia were developed as if no bomb were in the offing. Subsequent awareness of the significance of atomic weapons for the fate of mankind cannot alter this fact.

President Roosevelt by 1945 had abandoned his original expectation that China was capable of fulfilling the responsibilities of a great power, one of the Four Policemen, immediately after the defeat of Japan. He bowed before the incontestable evidence of the military weakness, economic chaos, and political bungling of Chiang Kai-shek's Nationalist regime. Once the President had dreamed of a new democratic and anticolonial order in Asia under Chinese leadership, but by the time of the Yalta conference he saw that China might not survive as a nation, much less assume leadership, unless the war with Japan was ended quickly and genuine cooperation established between the Chinese Nationalists and Communists. The President's military advisers said that the first condition required massive Russian military help—at least sixty divisions to attack the Japanese in Manchuria and north China, in General MacArthur's opinion. Similarly, the political goal of a peacefully unified China seemed impossible without support from Moscow.

The lowered American opinion of China's military and political capabilities was accompanied by an exaggerated estimate of Japan's power and willingness to prolong the war. Although a few military planners thought that Japan could be forced to surrender by bombardment and blockade of the home islands, the dominant opinion in the winter of 1945 was that victory could be achieved only by a large-scale invasion culminating in a great battle on the Tokyo plain eighteen months after the defeat of Germany which was predicted to take place between July 1 and December 31, 1945. Thus, victory over Japan was planned for the end of 1946 at the earliest and mid-1947 at the latest. It was impossible to estimate probable losses in this operation, but some guesses, based on the suicidal ferocity of the defense which the Japanese were then putting up in their Pacific outposts, ran as high as one million American casualties with Japanese losses running many times higher. The President was told repeatedly that early Russian intervention against the Japanese on the mainland was the only way to reduce such appalling losses. Little weight was given to the devastation being wrought on the Japanese economy by American air and naval attacks. Furthermore, no allowance was made for the possible use of the atomic bomb.

In retrospect it is clear that the estimates of early 1945 were unrealistically pessimistic. But at the time it seemed wiser to exaggerate the enemy's strength than to face disaster by erring in the opposite direction, as had happened to the British and Americans in 1941–1942. Who, after Pearl Harbor and Japan's continued success in China, was prepared to say the cost of victory would be light? Who, after Japan's record of perfidy in international relations, was prepared to see anything but further trickery in the occasional hints that came indirectly from Tokyo that Japan was ready for peace? Absolute insistence on unconditional surrender and an adamant refusal to be drawn into any discussion with the enemy were considered the only course for the United States to follow.

On the basis of this dark outlook, the secret agreement on the Far East which Roosevelt negotiated with Stalin at Yalta seemed highly advantageous to the United States and to China. The Soviet Uunion promised to enter the war against Japan "in two or three months after Germany has surrendered," and by separate agreement the United States confirmed its promise to supply huge quantities of equipment for the Russian forces in the Far East. Stalin also expressed his "readiness to conclude with the National Government of China a pact of friendship and alliance between the U.S.S.R. and China in order to render assistance to China for the purpose of liberating China from the Japanese yoke." In the optimistic atmosphere of Yalta, where the United States took much on faith, Americans interpreted this to mean that Russia would support the Nationalists as the postwar government of China and would not back the Chinese Communists. Stalin, after all, had several times expressed his low opinion of the Chinese Communists. The carefully qualified words of the Yalta accord, however, constituted no such promise.

In return Russia was granted the desires that Stalin had outlined at different times during the previous two years. Russia would get the Kurile Islands and the southern part of Sakhalin directly from Japan. Outer Mongolia, claimed by China as part of her territory, was to remain under Russian control in the form of the allegedly independent Mongolian People's Republic. Russia's "pre-eminent interests" in the principal ports and railroads of Manchuria were to be recognized and safeguarded through vaguely defined arrangements which reminded the historically minded of old-style sphere-of-influence imperialism. This impression was not weakened by the agreement's imprecise and contradictory assurance "that China shall retain full sovereignty in Manchuria."[1]

Chiang Kai-shek was not informed of the extensive concessions that Roosevelt made to Russia at China's expense, a fact

---

[1] U. S. Department of State, *Foreign Relations, The Conferences at Malta and Yalta, 1945* (Washington: U. S. Government Printing Office, 1955), p. 984.

which subsequently became a major item in the indictment advanced by critics of Roosevelt's diplomacy. At the time secrecy seemed justified by the need to prevent Japan from learning of Russia's intention of entering the war in Asia and by the conviction that no secrets were safe in Chinese hands. President Roosevelt was committed, however, to obtaining Chiang Kai-shek's approval of the Russian claims at a time designated by Stalin. This implied that the United States would support Russia in the event of a dispute with China over the precise meaning of the ambiguous document. Each of the Big Three signed the accord, although Churchill did so against the advice of Foreign Secretary Eden. The Prime Minister later excused himself by saying that he had not participated in drawing up the agreement and that he had no wish to interfere in an area which was the primary responsibility of the United States.

No significant changes occurred in the Far Eastern outlook in the two-month interval between the Yalta conference and President Roosevelt's death on April 12. President Truman had no choice but to continue along the general lines of Roosevelt's Asian policies while trying to learn about matters which had been kept secret from him until the moment of his becoming President. The reports that Truman received about Asia during his first weeks in office were conflicting, but predominantly optimistic in regard to Russian intentions. Most advisers believed that the Yalta accord remained a satisfactory basis for further diplomacy. For example, Patrick Hurley, the American ambassador to China, visited Churchill in London and Stalin in Moscow during the week of Roosevelt's death and reported that Stalin was in unqualified agreement with the American policy of seeking the peaceful unification of the feuding Chinese factions under the leadership of Chiang Kai-shek. On the other hand, Hurley suspected that the British, notwithstanding their professed agreement with the American objective, inwardly hoped for a weak and disunited China in order to preserve their hold on Hong Kong and their general imperial position in Asia.

Hurley's happy report was confirmed six weeks later by Harry Hopkins who, it will be recalled, was sent by Truman to see Stalin in preparation for the approaching Big Three meeting. Stalin reaffirmed for Hopkins his devotion to the ideal of a unified China under Chiang Kai-shek, and said that he would welcome a visit from Chinese Foreign Minister T. V. Soong in order to draw up a Sino-Soviet treaty. Furthermore, he would allow representatives of the Nationalist government to enter Manchuria with the Red Army. Stalin added that "the United States must play the largest part in helping China to get on their feet; the Soviet Union would be occupied with its own internal reconstruction and Great Britain would be occupied elsewhere." He also said that the Soviet Union supported the American idea of the Open Door of commercial nondiscrimination for all nations in China.[2] Hopkins was delighted.

If Hurley and Hopkins were right, there was no Far Eastern problem. Russia would attack Japan in August after amicably negotiating a treaty with the Chinese Nationalist government based on the Yalta accord. As the Japanese were rapidly expelled, representatives of the Nationalist government would assume the civil administration of China. The Communists, belittled by Stalin and lacking Soviet support, would have no choice but to accept Chiang Kai-shek's leadership. China, under American tutelage and open to American trade, would at last begin the climb toward unity, democracy, and prosperity. But this latest version of the century-old China dream was sharply challenged by some officials in Washington, most notably by Joseph C. Grew, acting Secretary of State while Stettinius headed the American delegation at the San Francisco conference. Taking note of the pattern of Soviet behavior in Europe, Grew in May 1945 predicted ominously that "the Far East will in due course be brought into the same pattern. Once Russia is in the war against Japan, then Mongolia, Manchuria, and Korea will gradually slip into Russia's orbit. . . . As soon as the San Francisco Conference is over," he urged, "'our policy toward Soviet Russia should immediately stiffen, all along the line.'"[3]

Other officials in the State Department with long experience in Far Eastern affairs were not as ominous in their recommenda-

---

[2] *Foreign Relations, Potsdam,* Vol. 1, p. 45.

[3] Joseph C. Grew, *Turbulent Era: A Diplomatic Record of Forty Years, 1904–1945,* Vol. 2 (Boston: Houghton Mifflin, 1952), p. 1446. Quotation used with the permission of the Houghton Mifflin Company.

tions as Grew, but they did urge the United States to intervene emphatically on China's side in the negotiations with Russia over the Yalta agreement. President Truman at the Potsdam conference was aware of disagreement among his advisers on the proper policy for the United States to follow toward Russia in the Far East, but he was not yet ready to undertake a complete reversal of the Rooseveltian approach. His eye was on victory which might come at any moment thanks to the staggering success of the atomic bomb, tested for the first time on July 16, the day before the Potsdam conference.

From the beginning of the vast project to develop an atomic bomb, all concerned took it for granted that the weapon would be used if it would shorten the war and save lives. From 1942 onward, however, many of the scientists on the project became increasingly concerned over the postwar role of the new weapon. Certain that Russia had the scientific capability to develop the bomb within a very short time (four years after the United States was a common estimate), they foresaw a potentially catastrophic arms race unless atomic energy was placed under effective international control. But the scientists had difficulty attracting sustained attention from President Roosevelt to their views. Instead, Roosevelt appeared to be thinking in terms of an Anglo-American atomic monopoly and during the war went further than his scientific advisers deemed wise in sharing atomic information and control with Great Britain. In the most important of several agreements, Roosevelt and Churchill promised on August 19, 1943 at the first Quebec conference that neither the United States nor Britain would use the weapon against each other, or against the enemy without the other's consent, or would give atomic information without the other's consent to other powers. Some scientists thought that this British veto on American decisions was dangerous in the light of Churchill's predilection for erecting a new balance of power against Russia. They did not want the United States to be harnessed to a British anti-Soviet policy after the war, and hoped for full freedom to initiate Soviet-American cooperation as the essential ingredient for international control which seemed the only way to save the world from destruction.

Failing to win Roosevelt's effective support for postwar planning, the scientists appealed to Henry L. Stimson who, as Secretary of War, was the cabinet member directly responsible for the development of the bomb. Stimson was responsive, but his heavy burdens and great age (he was 78 in 1945) plus the distraction of Roosevelt's death, delayed the convening of a broad interdepartmental policy group under Stimson's direction, known as the "Interim Committee," until May 9, two days after the surrender of Germany.

Within three months the bomb would be ready for use against Japan. At the same time, Russia, if true to the Yalta timetable, would enter the Asian war. In the few short weeks remaining before Truman's meeting with Stalin in July, it was necessary for the Interim Committee and the government as a whole to reach a cluster of momentous interconnected decisions. Although a few planners were primarily concerned with the need to arrange for international postwar control of the bomb, Stimson, Truman, and their closest advisers believed that every question was subordinate to the necessity of ending the war as quickly and bloodlessly as possible. The bomb, despite its awful implications for the future of mankind, had to be considered first as a means toward that immediate end.

Several times it was suggested—most articulately by a group of scientists associated with the atomic laboratory at the University of Chicago—that it was wrong to drop the bomb on Japan without giving the country warning and a chance to surrender. Several schemes for demonstrating the bomb—for example, on an uninhabited Pacific island with neutral observers —were put forward and rejected. Those responsible for the ultimate decision argued that a demonstration might not work, in which case the United States would stand accused of a bluff. Even if it did work, there was slight assurance that the Japanese government would be moved to surrender. On the contrary, they might interpret the tactic as a sign of American war weariness and redouble their resistance in an effort to win a negotiated peace. The only way to use the bomb, it was generally agreed, was against a major industrial city with a high concentration of workers' homes.

Closely related to the decision against a prior demonstration of the bomb was the issue of how, if at all, to give further definition to the meaning of unconditional surrender for Japan. Stimson and acting Secretary of State Grew were the leading exponents of the view that the Japanese should be told explicitly what to expect. Disarmament, loss of conquered territory, and the eradication of militarism—yes. National destruction, individual enslavement, or a denial of political self-determination— no. Specifically, they said that the Japanese should be assured that they could retain the institution of the Emperor, if they so chose. Grew, Stimson, and others contended that the Emperor would serve as a necessary symbol of authority, a stabilizing influence which would help the Japanese people become reconciled to defeat. Without an assurance on the Emperor, they argued, the Japanese might find it psychologically impossible to surrender and would fight on with heavy loss of life. Even with the use of the atomic bomb and Russian entry into the war, it would then prove necessary to undertake the bloody invasion which everyone now hoped to avoid. Significantly, American military planners strongly supported the proposal to let the Emperor remain.

The idea was opposed by James F. Byrnes, who replaced Stettinius as Secretary of State on July 3, and other officials who were more sensitive to American public opinion than knowledgeable in regard to Japan. They said that Japanese militarists might continue to exploit the throne as they had in the past. Furthermore, the American people would not understand and would rebuke any indication that the government was departing from the stern formula of unconditional surrender. Truman followed Byrnes—who was himself being powerfully influenced by former Secretary of State Hull—on this crucial point. When a warning, known as the Potsdam Declaration, was issued to Japan by Truman, Churchill, and Chiang Kai-shek on July 26, there was no hint that the Japanese people might be allowed to retain the Emperor, although they were assured economic sustenance and freedom of speech, religion, and thought. The government of Japan was given the stark alternative of unconditional surrender or "prompt and utter destruction."[4]

The Potsdam Declaration reached the Japanese government in the midst of an agonizing debate over whether and how to end the war. Since the beginning of the year a peace party had been gaining influence with the cabinet, but the diehard views of the military leaders were still powerful in July notwithstanding the fact that Japan's power for continued resistance was at an end. Reason demanded surrender, but the apparent likelihood that the United States would abolish the monarchy was an insurmountable obstacle for the advocates of peace. Forlornly and indecisively they sought Russian help in bringing about a conditional surrender, but they received a curt rebuff from Moscow. Stalin had his own plans. Truman knew of these Japanese overtures, but he interpreted them as a deceitful attempt to divide Russia from the United States at the moment of victory. When the Japanese Prime Minister seemed to dismiss the Potsdam warning with arrogant contempt, Truman was confirmed in his belief that only the atomic bomb could make Japan face reality. Would the Japanese government have surrendered before the dropping of the bomb if the Potsdam Declaration had contained a clause permitting the retention of the Emperor? Probably not, if we assume that the bomb would have fallen on August 6. If we assume a double "if": an assurance on the Emperor and the patience to hold back on the bomb while the Japanese cabinet went through the final agonies of debate, it does seem probable that Japan would have surrendered before many weeks had passed, probably before the November 1 invasion date set by the American military planners. But there is little profit in lingering too long over these might-have-beens.

Meanwhile, Truman at Potsdam had faced the question of how and when to tell Stalin of the new weapon. One alternative was to give the Russians detailed advance notice of the bomb and to take the initiative in proposing international control. The other extreme was to keep silent and let Russia draw her own conclusions by observing what the bomb did to Japan.

---

[4] For the final text of this much-revised document, see *Foreign Relations, Potsdam*, Vol. 2, pp. 1474–1476.

Truman selected an intermediate approach. On July 24, eight days after the Alamogordo test, he casually remarked to Stalin after a formal session of the conference had adjourned that the United States had a new weapon of unprecedented power. Stalin appeared unimpressed and simply replied that he hoped the United States would make good use of it against Japan.

The President's deliberate reticence reflected his rapidly ebbing patience toward the Soviets in general and in particular a new distrust of Russian intentions in the Far East. Sino-Soviet treaty negotiations were then in abeyance because Stalin was insisting on concessions going even beyond what had been granted in the Yalta accord; in effect the Russians were demanding complete control of Manchuria. Truman was reluctant to see the United States become deeply involved in this Sino-Soviet quarrel, but neither was he prepared, as Roosevelt might have been, to seek Russian cooperation in one area by a show of unsolicited generosity in another. Whether or not the President lost an opportunity at Potsdam to lay the foundations of international control over atomic weapons is another of those controversial questions that can never be settled. With the Soviets showing latent hostility on several fronts, the time did not seem ripe for such a gesture. Furthermore, Truman wanted to wind up the conference and get back to the United States. There had been too much talk already from his point of view.

The Postdam conference ended on August 2, 1945 and President Truman headed quickly home. While on board ship in mid-Atlantic he learned of the successful atomic bombing of Hiroshima. By prearrangement a short announcement in the President's name was released to the world: a bomb equivalent to more than 20,000 tons of TNT had been dropped. "It is a harnessing of the basic power of the universe." If Japan's leaders do not now surrender, he said, "they may expect a rain of ruin from the air, the like of which has never been seen on this earth." The President added that he would soon recommend to Congress the establishment of a "commission to control the production and use of atomic power within the United States." He avoided a direct comment on the issue of international control, which some men thought was the only way to achieve the survival of mankind, but he did promise to "give further consideration and make further recommendations to the Congress as to how atomic power can become a powerful and forceful influence towards the maintenance of world peace."[5]

The bomb set off a string of political decisions in Tokyo and Moscow. The disintegration of the country's communications prevented the government in Tokyo from learning in detail of Hiroshima for twenty-four hours. But on August 7, the Prime Minister advised the Emperor to accept the Potsdam Declaration. The military leaders, however, belittled the power of the bomb and sent an investigating team to Hiroshima. On the same day the Sino-Soviet negotiations, stalled because of Stalin's harsh demands on China, resumed in Moscow. Quickly the Soviets decided it was time to enter the war against Japan even though China had not yet agreed to Russia's terms. On the eighth the Japanese ambassador to Moscow was told that Russia, allegedly in response to a request from her allies, would consider herself at war on the ninth. At that moment Russian divisions were poised for a lightning advance into Manchuria and north China. The Russian decision stunned the diehards in the Japanese cabinet, but still the government in Tokyo was unable to reach a decision. The dropping of the second atomic bomb on Nagasaki, on August 9, did not break the deadlock. But in the early morning hours of the tenth, Emperor Hirohito accepted the unprecedented request of the peace faction that he make the decision personally. Hirohito declared that Japan must surrender, subject only to the preservation of his own sovereignty as Emperor. After the cabinet agreed, the Japanese decision was conveyed via neutral Switzerland to the United States.

The Japanese message forced Truman to make a difficult decision. Should Japan be allowed to surrender on condition that

---

[5] Harry S. Truman, Memoirs, Vol. 1, Year of Decisions (Garden City, N. Y.: Doubleday, 1955), pp. 422–423; and Herbert Feis, Japan Subdued: The Atomic Bomb and the End of the War in the Pacific (Princeton, N. J.: Princeton University Press, 1961), p. 111.

the Emperor be retained? Stimson and Leahy said yes. Byrnes
said no. Forrestal suggested that the Emperor be allowed to remain on the throne, but that his authority be subject to the
supreme commander of the Allied powers. Truman approved,
as did Great Britain, China, and Russia (after a slight delay).
On the eleventh Japan was so informed. A final struggle took
place within the Japanese government. A minority, led by the
War Minister, urged the country to hold out for better conditions. But Emperor Hirohito, for the second time making a
crucial decision personally, said Japan would surrender on American terms. On August 14 the Emperor's decision was relayed
to the Allied governments, and shortly thereafter broadcast
to the Japanese people. The war was over.

The remaining days of August were crowded. China and Russia signed (at midnight, August 14) a set of agreements defining
Russia's gains in Asia. The Chinese reluctantly gave Stalin what
he sought, and in return took comfort from the fact that the
Russians agreed not to support the Chinese Communists against
the Nationalist government. Having achieved their desires in
China, the Russians, whose war against Japan had lasted for
five days, sought a share equal to the United States in the control of occupied Japan and were brusquely rebuffed by President
Truman. Occupied Japan was placed under the sole authority
of General MacArthur, as commander of the Allied forces. The
other Allies, including Russia, subsequently enjoyed a nominal
right to give advice. In practice, this meant nothing. Japan was
an American show, and the director was MacArthur.

China presented a greater, indeed an insoluble, problem from
the American point of view. All Japanese troops within China
were directed to surrender to Chiang Kai-shek while troops in
Manchuria and Korea, north of 38 degrees north latitude, were
to surrender to the Russians. But Chiang lacked the transportation to carry his armies into the vast areas of northern and
eastern China where the Japanese were ready to surrender.
Meanwhile, the China Communists were advancing rapidly,
accepting the surrender of Japanese troops and building a large
supply of captured weapons. The Japanese commanders could
be, and were, instructed to surrender only to the Nationalists,
but instructions were meaningless if the Chinese Communists

were on hand and the Nationalists were immobilized hundreds of miles away. General Albert C. Wedemeyer, American commanding general in China, believed it was essential for the United States to devote every possible resource in men and equipment to carrying the Nationalist troops north and eastward. Wedemeyer's plans were accepted in Washington in principle, but subject to two crippling qualifications: he was to receive only two divisions and these not until all the needs of General MacArthur in Japan were satisfied; and he was to take no action that might involve American troops in the conflict between the Chinese Nationalists and Communists. Thus, at a critical moment, the transfer of Nationalist troops proceeded with exasperating slowness. Every passing day brought an increase in Chinese Communist power. Late in the year 1945 the American government intensified its efforts to arrange a peaceful settlement between Communists and Nationalists, but to no avail. The combination of Communist strength and Nationalist blunders had by then created a situation in which an eventual Communist triumph in China was virtually inevitable.

CHAPTER X

The Legacy of Victory

In terms of the assumptions which had sustained the national war effort since the day of Pearl Harbor, victory lay gloriously complete. Hitler was dead and Germany lay powerless under Allied occupation. The Emperor's decision to surrender meant that the landings on Japan would be bloodless. Italy, ineffectual minor partner of the Axis, had withdrawn from the war two years before and, having repudiated fascism, was about to acquire a respected place among nations. The temptation was great during those happy August days of 1945 to dwell on the achievements of the nation in battle, on the home front, and around the diplomatic conference table. Americans, virtually unaided, had beaten Japan in the Pacific while providing the leadership and more than half the men for the attack on Hitler from the West. At the same time they had armed Britain, Russia, and China. Their diplomacy had preserved the great coalition, established the United Nations, and laid foundations for peace in Europe and Asia.

No informed American, however, could give in to that temptation. There was far too much evidence that the legacy of victory was not peace and prosperity for all mankind—as the Atlantic Charter had promised—but continued suffering, hatred, and threat of war. The United States directly and by supporting its allies had encompassed the unconditional defeat of the Axis enemy, but now found itself in a world where there was less national security than in 1941. Roosevelt and his advisers had correctly foreseen that genuine peace and security were impossible without firm Soviet-Western cooperation. They had followed tactics of conciliation and well-meaning appeasement of Russia during the war, but failed to win anything but a few paper agreements. By late summer 1945 even the paper agreements were in tatters. Little remained to conceal Soviet Russia's fundamental hostility to the non-Communist world.

For a few months longer American leaders in their public statements refrained from giving full voice to their somber conclusions, but privately most of them recognized that what was soon to be called "the Cold War" had begun. Behind the "Iron Curtain" the Russians were ruthlessly suppressing democracy, as it was understood in the West, and were erecting a cordon of Communist satellites: Poland, Hungary, Rumania, Bulgaria. Yugoslavia, if not a satellite under Tito, was closely tied to Moscow and a threat to peace through its territorial claims against Italy at the head of the Adriatic. Events in these countries were the subject of long and tedious argument at Potsdam. The United States and Britain complained that Russia was ignoring the Yalta agreements. Western observers in Russian-dominated areas were being denied freedom of movement and inquiry. Russia was acting unilaterally without the consultation promised at Yalta. Free elections were not being held; and (a minor complaint) American and British private property within the countries was being confiscated. Stalin and Molotov were so unmoved by these complaints that they scarcely bothered to justify Russia's behavior.

Germany, under four-power occupation, was already becoming a battleground in the Cold War rather than the symbol of Allied unity which the well-intentioned had hoped. President Truman at the Potsdam conference urged that Germany be treated as an economic unit, but Anglo-American efforts to work out genuinely uniform policies with Russia came to naught. In theory all three great powers had abandoned their wartime schemes for the dismemberment of Germany, but in fact the boundary dividing the Russian from the British and American zones had already severed the country. Furthermore, Russia had unilaterally turned over a large area of eastern Germany to Poland in defiance of Western protests. Berlin, an enclave in the Russian zone, was divided like Germany as a whole into four zones. Western access rights to the city had still not been defined by formal agreement. Austria, which by agreement was to be restored as an independent country, was like Germany divided into four zones of occupation (Vienna being treated in a manner similar to Berlin) and was also a medium of discord rather than cooperation.

Economically, all of Europe was prostrate. The United States was supplying food for temporary relief through the United Nations Relief and Rehabilitation Administration (UNRRA), but the American government and people had not yet faced the political implications of the possible spread of Communism into a dispirited and impoverished western Europe. Roosevelt had assumed that the American people would be unwilling to keep troops in Europe more than two years after victory or take on any long-term economic burdens. Although this assumption had not been publicly challenged by the late summer of 1945, an increasing number of observers were beginning to feel that American security demanded the very things which Roosevelt had assumed were impossible.

The legacy of victory was equally grim in Asia. There would be no friction with Russia in Japan because Truman had figuratively told Stalin to go to hell when he asked to share the control of the occupied country. Korea, however, was about to become a focal point of Soviet-American tension. Divided into occupation zones along the thirty-eighth parallel, it was in some respects an Asian equivalent of Germany. By 1950 Communist China had replaced Russia as the controlling power in North Korea and the United States found itself fighting a costly war simply to preserve the status quo of partition. Meanwhile, China's problems defied solution with the limited means which the United States was ready to apply. Few knowledgeable men really believed that exhortation would bring about the peaceful unification of Chiang Kai-shek's regime with the Chinese Communists. But for a nation unwilling to risk lives and large sums of money, exhortation was the only tactic available. It failed utterly. In 1949 the Chinese Communists gained complete control of the mainland when Chiang Kai-shek's Nationalist government retreated to Formosa, the crowded island which in accordance with the Cairo declaration of 1943 had been taken from Japan.

The early wartime assumption concerning Nationalist China's ability to bring leadership and stability to Asia was forgotten by 1945, but no new, workable premise had arisen in its place.

In like manner, the determination to encourage the elimination of European colonialism from Asia had grown weaker without leading to a new policy for the colonial areas. The desire of American military leaders to retain unqualified national control for strategic reasons of islands in the Pacific was a major factor in this retreat from dogmatic anticolonialism. Thus, the United States emerged from the war with a vast collection of what were in effect Pacific island colonies, Okinawa being the largest and most important. On the other hand, the Philippines gained their independence in 1946 in accordance with earlier promises. Hong Kong was returned to British sovereignty, notwithstanding Roosevelt's frequent suggestions that it should be given to the Chinese. The British also regained sovereignty over Burma and Malaya, although both colonies were put on the road to independence as were the Netherlands East Indies. After the unsuccessful wartime intervention in British-Indian relations, the United States kept hands off India. The British Labour government moved quickly to grant the independence that had been promised but their best efforts were unable to prevent a Moslem-Hindu bloodbath or the partition of the country. Indochina, once considered by Roosevelt for trusteeship under Chinese administration, reverted to France. The French attempt to grant autonomy within the French Union to the different countries of Indochina led to a bloody colonial war and defeat for France despite the ironic military support of the United States.

In the Middle East the American wartime objectives of liquidating British and French authority had been largely achieved, but the results—war over Palestine, anti-Western nationalism in Egypt, Syria, Iraq, and Iran, and generally an increase in Soviet prestige—were not what American idealists had hoped. As in other areas of the world, the United States had encouraged the eradication of old regimes without being able to devise alternatives that served the national interest. Ultimately, the United States felt obliged to assume heavy economic and military commitments in the Middle East with mixed and less than satisfactory results.

Even Latin America, the one region which in 1945 seemed securely within the orbit of American beneficence, proved in a short time to be a source of anti-American discontent and, through ties with the Communist world, of direct insecurity for the United States.

Over this dismal, variegated globe lay the shadow of annihilation cast by the discovery of nuclear explosives. In August 1945 the American government did not know how to deal with this unprecedented fact of technology which had so suddenly changed all the old conditions in which nations sought through war and diplomacy to gain advantage over one another. Some Americans thought the United States should hold its secret and openly use its new power to coerce Russia. Others said that this course would lead to mutual destruction on the not-too-distant day when Russia had her own nuclear weapons. The second group said that the United States should voluntarily relinquish its atomic monopoly to an international authority. Actual policy as developed in subsequent months followed middle ground: a proposal to preserve the American monopoly of weapons until an international authority with adequate provision for inspection against violation was established. The Soviet Union, apparently suspecting a trick and hard at work on its own nuclear research, said no. The nuclear arms race was under way.

One of the most somber aspects of the study of history is that it suggests no obvious ways by which mankind could have avoided folly. Would the postwar world have been a happier and more secure place for the United States and for all mankind if Roosevelt had behaved differently during the war? Possibly. It also might have been worse. Russia treated as an adversary rather than friend might, as men feared at the time, have reached a truce with Hitler. This seems unlikely, but the possibility was there. Or Stalin in the face of the type of opposition which Churchill recommended in 1945 might have acted with less rather than more restraint in Europe and Asia. Who knows?

The critic who denounces Roosevelt as a fool or worse and then says that such-and-such an alternative strategy in Europe and Asia, or both, would have altered the world for the better can never be convincing. In fairness to Roosevelt and his advisers, all that can be said is that they held too long to stereotypes about the United States and other nations and that they acted too often on the basis of hopes and illusion rather than ascertainable fact. If, as most men believe, it is usually wiser to base policies on as much fact as possible, then American leaders during the war were misguided. But even in saying this, one must be aware of the obstacles which stood in the way of finding facts and acting upon them during the war. Stereotypes are hard enough to avoid in ordinary times when men are free to reflect carefully about the world confronting them.

At the root of many American wartime stereotypes was a tendency to think about unfamiliar areas of the world in terms of historical analogies drawn from American experience. For example, Roosevelt knew very little about India but did not hesitate to suggest that Indians should imitate the history of the United States in the era of eighteenth-century struggle for independence from England. Similarly, the tendency to assume that other people and nations behaved like Americans prevented wartime leaders from understanding the depth of the internal disputes which plagued Poland and China. The facile transferral of American assumptions also led to serious miscalculations when Soviet leaders used words like "democracy," "freedom," and "independence." The next step was to ignore Russian history and Communist ideology and simply take it for granted that Soviet Russia and the United States, because they used the same words and because they both desired the defeat of the Axis, had identical expectations for the future.

Americans also held stereotyped views concerning the enemy. Unconditional surrender undoubtedly was the soundest policy to apply toward Hitler's Germany, but the simplicity of this phrase made it difficult to think of Germany in constructive ways. Hitler had brought misery to the world, but this did not lessen the fact that Europe would depend on the contributions of the German economy. Similarly, one could condemn Japan for her aggression in Asia and her sneak attack on the United States, but the simple application of unconditional surrender provided no answer to how Japan's positive role in the Asian economy would be filled. In the specific decision to drop the atomic bomb it would appear that Americans were convinced of the alleged suicidal fanaticism of the Japanese people and were prevented from seeing that Japan was close to surrender.

Perhaps the most persistent illusion of the war pertained to the probable future behavior of the United States. President Roosevelt and many others were obsessed by the unhappy national experience of 1917–1920 which seemed to prove that the American people would not tolerate permanent involvement in foreign affairs if that involvement required heavy expenditures or the risk of lives. This memory inhibited Roosevelt from contemplating postwar situations which necessitated sustained American involvement outside the Western hemisphere. Under the general aegis of the United Nations, a cooperative Russia would maintain stability in Europe east of Germany. Britain would perform the same function in western Europe where France was likely to cause trouble according to Roosevelt's stereotype. In Asia China might some day attain responsibility, but meanwhile much would depend, as in Europe, on the cooperative spirit of Russia.

Wilson's experience also stimulated a fervent dedication to the establishment of the United Nations, as a redemption of the ideal League of Nations and a painless instrument for lasting world peace. The naive enthusiasm generated throughout the United States for the United Nations during 1945 diverted the public's attention from the multiple unsolved problems facing the nation. Excessive faith in the United Nations may also have contributed to subsequent disillusionment and denigration of the many useful but limited tasks which the world organization is capable of handling.

Reliance on these stereotypes simplified the task of wartime leadership for President Roosevelt, but added immeasurably to the tasks of his successors. Two decades after Roosevelt's death American leaders still find it necessary to explain that the permanent solutions to international problems, which were implicit in the rhetoric of the Second World War, do not exist and that the preservation of peace and national security is onerous, never-ending, and expensive. That story, however, belongs to the historians of the Cold War.

Suggestions for Additional Reading

One man in a lifetime could read only a small fraction of the vast and still rapidly growing literature on the Second World War. The titles here suggested for their direct bearing on American wartime diplomacy constitute the briefest introduction. Additional titles can be located conveniently in Henry L. Roberts, *Foreign Affairs Bibliography: A Selected and Annotated List of Books on International Relations, 1942–1952* (New York: Harper, 1955); Henry L. Roberts, *Foreign Affairs Bibliography, 1952–1962* (New York: Bowker, 1964); and in the quarterly issues of *Foreign Affairs*.

The asterisk indicates that a paperback edition is also available.

1. GENERAL WORKS

Every student of American diplomacy during the Second World War owes a debt to Herbert Feis whose massive *Churchill, Roosevelt, Stalin: The War They Waged and the Peace They Sought* (Princeton, N.J.: Princeton University Press, 1957) is the best account of the interaction of the Big Three from the entry of the United States into the war until the surrender of Germany. Feis's precise narrative is continued in *Between War and Peace: The Potsdam Conference* (Princeton, N.J.: Princeton University Press, 1960) and *Japan Subdued: The Atomic Bomb and the End of the War in the Pacific* (Princeton, N.J.: Princeton University Press, 1961). In another volume Feis describes *The China Tangle: The American Effort in China from Pearl Harbor to the Marshall Mission* (Princeton, N.J.: Princeton

University Press, 1953). For a balanced treatment of coalition diplomacy, see William H. McNeill, *America, Britain and Russia: Their Co-operation and Conflict, 1941–46* (London: Oxford University Press, 1953), a volume in the indispensable *Survey of International Affairs, 1939–46* issued by the Royal Institute of International Affairs under the general editorship of Arnold Toynbee. Sir Llewellyn Woodward's official history of *British Foreign Policy in the Second World War* (London: Her Majesty's Stationery Office, 1962) is a dry but important volume based on the records of the Foreign Office. John L. Snell, *Illusion and Necessity: The Diplomacy of Global War, 1939–1945* (Boston: Houghton Mifflin, 1963) is brief (229 pages) and particularly admirable for its attention to the diplomacy of the Axis and its bibliographical notes. Richard W. Leopold, *The Growth of American Foreign Policy* (New York: Knopf, 1962) treats the events of the war in broad historical context and also has a good bibliography. A. Russell Buchanan's *The United States and World War II* (2 vols., New York: Harper and Row, 1964)* treats primarily of military events.

The last four volumes of Winston S. Churchill's monumental *The Second World War* (6 vols., Boston: Houghton Mifflin, 1948–1953)* cover the period of American belligerency. They are: *The Grand Alliance* (1950), *Closing the Ring* (1951). *The Hinge of Fate* (1953), and *Triumph and Tragedy* (1953). These volumes, like their author, have no equals. Although no American memoirs approach Churchill's in grandeur, the most important are Robert E. Sherwood, *Roosevelt and Hopkins: An Intimate History* (New York: Harper, 1948)* and Cordell Hull, *The Memoirs of Cordell Hull* (2 vols., New York: Macmillan, 1948). Julius W. Pratt, *Cordell Hull* (2 vols., New York: Cooper Square, 1964),—Volumes 12 and 13 in *The American Secretaries of State and Their Diplomacy* edited by Samuel Flagg Bemis and Robert H. Ferrell—provides a gentle but necessary corrective to some points in Hull's *Memoirs*.

2. SPECIAL STUDIES

Short, provocative introductions to the connections between military strategy and diplomacy are provided by Hanson W.

Baldwin, *Great Mistakes of the War* (New York: Harper, 1950) which is somewhat overstated and Samuel E. Morison, *Strategy and Compromise* (Boston: Little, Brown, 1958) which is graceful. Also see the essay by William R. Emerson on "F.D.R." in Ernest R. May (Ed.), *The Ultimate Decision: The President as Commander in Chief* (New York: Braziller, 1960) and Kent Roberts Greenfield (Ed.), *Command Decisions* (Washington: U.S. Government Printing Office, 1960). Official historians have produced and are still producing dozens of fat and detailed tomes. The most significant for the student of diplomacy are Ray S. Cline, *Washington Command Post: The Operations Division* (1951); Forrest C. Pogue, *The Supreme Command* (1954); Maurice Matloff and Edwin M. Snell, *Strategic Planning for Coalition Warfare*, 1941–1942 (1953); Matloff alone, *Strategic Planning for Coalition Warfare*, 1943–44 (1959); and the three volumes by Charles F. Romanus and Riley Sunderland on *The China-Burma-India Theater* (1953–59)—all published in Washington (U.S. Government Printing Office) in the series on the *U.S. Army in World War II*. For the history of the U. S. Navy see Samuel E. Morison, *The Two-Ocean War* (Boston: Little, Brown, 1963) which presents the essence of his fifteen-volume *History of the United States Naval Operations in World War II*. See also John Ehrman's two volumes on *Grand Strategy, 1943–45* (London: Her Majesty's Stationery Office, 1956) in the British official military history of the war. Chester Wilmot, *The Struggle for Europe* (New York: Harper, 1952)* is a stimulating and critical general military history.

For German issues see: John L. Snell, *Wartime Origins of the East-West Dilemma Over Germany* (New Orleans: Hauser, 1959), a solid book; and Anne Armstrong, *Unconditional Surrender: The Impact of the Casablanca Policy upon World War II* (New Brunswick, N.J.: Rutgers University Press, 1961) which contains interesting material on the situation inside Germany but reaches debatable conclusions and is less comprehensive than its title suggests. Paul Kecskemeti, *Strategic Surrender: The Politics of Victory and Defeat* (Stanford, Calif.: Stanford University Press, 1958)* is an interesting study of the surrenders of France in 1940, Italy in 1943, Germany in 1945, and Japan in 1945 in terms of political theory. John L. Snell (Ed.), *The*

Meaning of Yalta (Baton Rouge: Louisiana State University Press, 1956) is a convenient primer on the major issues under discussion at that conference. On American policy toward France see: William L. Langer, *Our Vichy Gamble* (New York: Knopf, 1947) and Arthur L. Funk, *Charles de Gaulle: The Crucial Years, 1943–44* (Norman, Okla.: University of Oklahoma Press, 1959). On Italy: Norman Kogan, *Italy and the Allies* (Cambridge, Mass.: Harvard University Press, 1956). For Spain and Portugal see Arnold Toynbee (Ed.), *Survey of International Affairs, 1939–1946: The War and the Neutrals* (London: Oxford University Press, 1956) and Herbert Feis, *The Spanish Story: Franco and the Nations at War* (New York: Knopf, 1948). For Poland and eastern Europe see Arnold Toynbee (Ed.), *Survey of International Affairs, 1939–1946: The Realignment of Europe* (London: Oxford University Press, 1955); Edward J. Rozek, *Allied Wartime Diplomacy: A Pattern in Poland* (New York: Wiley, 1958) which is contentious but important for its extensive quotations from the private papers of Prime Minister Stanislow Mikolajczyk; Fitzroy Maclean, *The Heretic: The Life and Times of Josip Broz-Tito* (New York: Harper, 1957) by the chief British liaison officer with Tito during the war; and Robert L. Wolff, *The Balkans in Our Time* (Cambridge, Mass.: Harvard University Press, 1956). George Kirk's *The Middle East in the War* (London: Oxford University Press, 1952) in the *Survey of International Affairs, 1939–1946* is the best book on that subject; see also the section on Turkey in *The War and the Neutrals* and Lewis V. Thomas and Richard N. Frye, *The United States and Turkey and Iran* (Cambridge, Mass.: Harvard University Press, 1951). Frank E. Manuel, *The Realities of American-Palestine Relations* (Washington: Public Affairs Press, 1949) is a relatively objective exception to the generally subjective literature on the Palestine problem. There is no single outstanding work devoted to the relations of the United States and Latin America during the war, but see Donald M. Dozer, *Are We Good Neighbors? Three Decades of Inter-American Relations, 1930–1960* (Gainesville, Fla.: University of Florida Press, 1959). For Asia see Feis, *The China Tangle* and *Japan Subdued* (above); F. C. Jones, *Japan's New Order in East Asia: Its Rise and Fall, 1937–1945* (London: Oxford University Press, 1954) and F. C. Jones and others, *The Far East*,

1942–1946 (London: Oxford University Press, 1955) in the *Survey of International Affairs, 1939–1946,* a balanced and comprehensive volume; Tang Tsou, *America's Failure in China, 1941–1950* (Chicago: University of Chicago Press, 1963), a fascinatingly detailed study by a political scientist; and Robert J. C. Butow, *Japan's Decision to Surrender* (Stanford, Calif.: Stanford University Press, 1954). On the atomic bomb: Leslie R. Groves, *Now It Can Be Told* (New York: Harper, 1962) by the general in command of the Manhattan Project; and the very important first volume in the official history of the Atomic Energy Commission by Richard G. Hewlett and Oscar E. Anderson, *The New World, 1939–1946* (University Park, Pa.: Pennsylvania State University Press, 1962). Louis Morton has written a thoughtful summary of the factors bearing on "The Decision to Use the Atomic Bomb," pp. 493–518 in Greenfield (Ed.), *Command Decisions* (above). On wartime planning for the United Nations, see two excellent books: Ruth B. Russell, *A History of the United Nations Charter: The Role the United States, 1940–45* (Washington: Brookings Institution, 1958) and the Department of State, *Postwar Foreign Policy Preparation* (Washington: U.S. Government Printing Office, 1950) written by Harley Notter (whose name for some odd reason is not on the title page). Lloyd C. Gardner's *Economic Aspects of New Deal Diplomacy* (Madison, Wis.: University of Wisconsin Press, 1964) is an important and original study.

3. MEMOIRS AND BIOGRAPHIES

Of several hundred memoirs and biographies of leading wartime figures, the following are some of the more important for the student of American diplomacy. All memoirs, however, should be used with caution, for their authors tend to have vague, inaccurate, and selective memories; many write from an exceedingly narrow and some from a prejudiced point of view. It is wise never to accept completely an uncorroborated statement in a memoir. For the Presidency, Harry S. Truman's *Memoirs,* Vol. 1, *Year of Decisions* (Garden City, N.Y.: Doubleday, 1955) belongs next to Sherwood's *Roosevelt and Hopkins.* For American State Department officials and civilian envoys, in addition to *The Memoirs of Cordell Hull,* see: Sumner Welles,

Seven Decisions That Shaped History (New York: Harper, 1951), a justification of his own and President Roosevelt's policies; Edward R. Stettinius, Jr., *Roosevelt and the Russians: The Yalta Conference*, edited by Walter Johnson (Garden City, N.Y.: Doubleday, 1949), an apologia containing a few details not available elsewhere; James F. Byrnes, *Speaking Frankly* (New York: Harper, 1947) and *All in One Lifetime* (New York: Harper, 1958) for their chapters on Yalta and Potsdam; Robert Murphy, *Diplomat Among Warriors* (Garden City, N.Y.: Doubleday, 1964), an important book especially for the author's role in relations with Vichy France and defeated Italy; Joseph C. Grew, *Turbulent Era* (2 vols., Boston: Houghton Mifflin, 1952), the concluding chapters of which relate to the author's work as Under and Acting Secretary of State during 1945 and especially to the question of Japan's surrender; William Phillips, *Ventures in Diplomacy* (Portland, Me.: Author, 1952) for the author's mission to India in 1943; William H. Standley and Arthur A. Ageton, *Admiral Ambassador to Russia* (Chicago: Regnery, 1955); and Carlton J. H. Hayes, *Wartime Mission in Spain, 1942–45* (New York: Macmillan, 1945). One of the most important sources for American wartime policy is Henry L. Stimson and McGeorge Bundy, *On Active Service in Peace and War* (New York: Harper, 1948), the second half of which deals with Stimson's service as Secretary of War, 1940–1945. See also Elting E. Morison, *Turmoil and Tradition: A Study of the Life and Times of Henry L. Stimson* (Boston: Houghton Mifflin, 1960). Walter Millis (Ed.), *The Forrestal Diaries* (New York: Viking, 1951) reveals the strong opinions of the Secretary of the Navy during the final year of the war. The only important memoir of a wartime leader in Congress is Arthur H. Vandenberg, Jr. (Ed.), *The Private Papers of Senator Vandenberg* (Boston: Houghton Mifflin, 1952). Senator Tom Connally's *My Name Is Tom Connally* (New York: Crowell, 1954) is thin.

Military memoirs and biographies abound: For General Dwight D. Eisenhower see his *Crusade in Europe* (Garden City, N. Y.: Doubleday, 1948) and Harry C. Butcher, *My Three Years with Eisenhower* (New York: Simon and Schuster, 1946) by Eisenhower's naval aide, 1942-1945. For the U. S. naval commander-in-chief see Ernest J. King and Walter Muir Whitehill, *Fleet Admiral King* (New York: Norton, 1952). Admiral William

D. Leahy's *I Was There* (New York: Whittlesey House, 1950) is less important as a source now than in 1950, but still contains details not available elsewhere. General Henry H. Arnold's *Global Mission* (New York: Harper, 1949) presents the point of view of the wartime chief of the Army Air Force. Joseph W. Stilwell, *The Stilwell Papers* (New York: Sloane Associates, 1948) is a salty and entertaining selection made by Theodore H. White of the diaries and letters of the commander of the China-Burma-India theater and pungent critic of Chiang Kai-shek. Albert C. Wedemeyer, *Wedemeyer Reports!* (New York: Holt, 1958) is agitated but important because the author was Stilwell's successor in China. John R. Deane, *The Strange Alliance: The Story of Our Efforts at Wartime Cooperation with Russia* (New York: Viking, 1947) is a revealing and authentic account by the head of the American military mission in Russia, 1943-1945.

Among important memoirs by foreign leaders are, in addition to Churchill's six volumes, Charles de Gaulle, *War Memoirs* (3 vols., New York: 1955-1960); Arthur Bryant, *The Turn of the Tide* and *Triumph in the West* (Garden City, N.Y.: Doubleday, 1957-1959), "a history of the war years based on the diaries of Field-Marshall Lord Alanbrooke, Chief of the Imperial General Staff"; and Stanislaw Mikolajczk, *The Rape of Poland* (New York: Whittlesey House, 1948).

4. DOCUMENTS

For the most part the documents which have appeared in print on wartime diplomacy are too scattered, incomplete, or tendentious to be of use to the nonspecialist. The one great exception is the Department of State's *Foreign Relations of the United States: Diplomatic Papers*. These carefully prepared volumes are currently appearing about twenty years after the events which they document. As of mid-1964 volumes for 1943 were appearing. In addition to the regular series covering the world by regions, there are the extremely important conference volumes. As of mid-1964 volumes had appeared for the Teheran, Yalta, and Potsdam (2 vols.) conferences. Few printed sources can give the reader a more detailed feel of the texture of wartime diplomacy than *Foreign Relations;* without them the present study could not have been written.

Index